LIFE BEYOND THE
AIRING CUPBOARD

The Cricket Society
and MCC
Book of the Year

LIFE BEYOND THE
AIRING CUPBOARD

JOHN BARCLAY

with a foreword by
Mike Atherton

illustrations by Susanna Kendall

FAIRFIELD BOOKS

Fairfield Books
17 George's Road, Bath BA1 6EY
Tel 01225-335813

First published 2008

ISBN: 978 0 9560702 0 3

Jacket design by Niall Allsop
from a painting by Renira Barclay

Printed and bound in Great Britain by
Midway Colour Print, Holt, Wiltshire

CONTENTS

to my mother Clare

I would like to thank the following for their encouragement and help:

Annabel Jordan, for coping with my scrawl and typing the manuscript,

my wife Renira for endless support, particularly with the difficult bits, and for painting the front cover,

Stephen Chalke and Susanna Kendall, for masterminding the project, and Susanna for her wonderful drawings which bring the text to life,

Mike Atherton, for opening the batting with his perceptive and entertaining foreword, and

my children Georgie and Theo, who have patiently read the text and only rarely irritated me with their comments.

FOREWORD

by Mike Atherton

It is a good thing that complete common ground is not a pre-requisite for friendship. If it was, readers of *Life beyond the Airing Cupboard* would quite properly wonder how John Barclay and I came to hit it off. As you will discover he is from an exotic and posh background (I lost count of the number of double-barrelled names that appear in the opening couple of chapters); he is at once depressive and incurably optimistic; he is deeply religious; he enjoys gardening and wildlife and all that kind of thing and he is, at heart, a romantic. I am none of those things.

There is some common ground, however: we like cricket and cricketers; we are inquisitive about the nature of that most peculiar form of wildlife – human beings – and we like fishing. The first two were common to us before we met. The last came as a result of our friendship, and readers are taken into this private world towards the end of this book when my incompetent thrashing around with rod and line is given a very public airing.

My association with John is a relatively recent one and our shared experiences take up the last quarter of the book. Given that these chapters involve quite high-profile events, calamitous England tours, troublesome England players (and coaches) and that sort of thing, this may be the part of the book that appeals to would-be readers. I hope not. Certainly, I had no wish to relive these events again and the publishing industry pays enough homage to this kind of thing anyway.

Rather, there is something of a lost world in the chapters before I and my England colleagues make an appearance that intrigued me and I hope will intrigue you. I'm talking about the era of professional cricket in England before it became, well, professional. John has touched on this theme before in his *The Appeal of the Championship* and this might be regarded as a charming sequel with a bit of autobiography tacked on.

This was a time when county cricket was allowed to be itself, to meander along without the apparent need to justify itself to the bean-counters. Pre-Thatcherite cricket, I suppose. It was also a game with infinite variety; John's struggles against Derek Underwood on a sticky-dog would be unfamiliar to a generation of batsmen weaned on dry surfaces and used to bullying spinners with sledge-hammer bats. There is no chance of the modern cricketer being able to recount, as John does here, practising his run-up and action in the middle of the night, tripping over his room-mate's feet so waking him up: cricketers may still practise their action in the still of the night, but they no longer share rooms.

None of this is to say that the modern game is any worse, just different. There is, though, a generation out there – the newspaper-reading, county-cricket loving generation – who, I suspect, regret some of the modern trends such as the move away from out-ground festivals, the move to the bland uniformity of four-day cricket and the absence, sometimes, of the kind of joy and schoolboy fun that infuses most of these pages. They will enjoy this book.

But there is a serious tone to these pages, too. Marcus Trescothick's recent autobiography is a reminder that depression can affect even those with the luckiest jobs. John's account of his demons is less brutal, less in-your-face than Trescothick's but all the more moving for that. I had no idea how badly John suffered and it is to cricket's credit that the likes of John and Marcus can talk more openly about their problems without worrying about the response. Cricket, thankfully, has entered a more mature age.

All the emotions we go through in life are here: the adolescent worries and fears, the hopes and dreams of youth; the joy and discovery of young love, both imagined (with a nanny on tour!) and real, and the pain and utter despair of losing the person you have loved. On page 80, John describes falling in love for the first time: 'true love,' he says, 'is a slow process, like second-class mail, filled with uncertainty and without the confidence that the end product will ever materialise.' The letter reached its destination but the post-master in the sky took it away far too soon.

Cricket helped ease the pain and what emerges from this book is that cricket is important, but only as a medium for development of the human spirit. And it is in this regard that John's most important work (beyond being a husband and a father), as head of a foundation that encourages children who would not have the opportunity to play at places like Arundel, continues.

This, then, is a life in cricket seen through the eyes of a man who admits towards the end of the book to preferring funerals to weddings. That, by the way, is another thing we have in common.

PREFACE BY THE AUTHOR

In February 2001, just two months after my wife Mary-Lou died, I was invited by Keith Blackmore, then Sports Editor of *The Times*, to submit a few cricketing sketches based around the 1981 summer, one of near success for Sussex and dramatic triumph for England in their encounter with Australia. To my surprise *The Times* published them through the summer of 2001 when once again England were locked in battle with Australia minus the success of twenty years earlier.

So inspired I was by this short-lived literary success that, with the help of Stephen Chalke, I created a book from the sketches, *The Appeal of the Championship*, which was well received and sold out.

In 2002 I wrote a fresh series of articles for *The Times*, mostly about cricketing events that had amused or interested me. Sadly this time they only had room for one of them. But, undaunted by this minor setback, I have completed the rest and added a few more for good measure. Once again with Stephen, I have turned them into a book about cricket – and many other things besides.

I have enormously enjoyed writing these stories; it's not hard to write about a subject that you love and with which you are slightly obsessed. Once a month I have met up with Stephen at Stockbridge in Hampshire. In the Grosvenor Hotel we have chatted about cricket and come up with ideas which have taken us far beyond the airing cupboard and into a more grown-up world. And all this a mere fifty yards from where I caught my first two-pound trout in the River Test back in 1968.

The life span of a professional cricketer is short but the repercussions long-lasting. I made my decision to retire quite suddenly after a particularly damaging defeat in the quarter-finals of the Benson & Hedges Trophy at Lord's against Middlesex. All day I had been tormented by Brearley, Edmonds, Emburey and Daniel, and by the end of it I knew I had had enough. When I got back home to Amberley later that evening and gave this news to Mary-Lou, the dog and cat in the kitchen, none of them seemed unduly surprised. If anything, they were relieved, and Mary-Lou brought me down to earth by saying, "Maturity at last."

1

THE AIRING CUPBOARD

The bell rang for break. Bottles of tepid milk with silver tops were handed out by a grumpy member of the kitchen staff who felt she had better things to do. It was early in the summer term 1964, when milk was considered to be good for us, that I first discovered the airing cupboard which both spared me from drinking the filthy stuff and provided me with my own space, in which I could think clearly and without disturbance.

Looking back, I can remember that, on Wednesdays and Saturdays when cricket matches were played at school, I would remove myself from the crowded classroom at the beginning of the mid-morning break and make a bee-line for the airing cupboard. Collecting my cricket bat – a Gray Nicolls Ted Dexter autograph – from the changing-room, I would firmly close the door and sit down on the laundry. Strange behaviour, you may think, but it meant so much to me and became an important, indeed essential, part of my preparation for cricket matches, even if it was not yet recommended in the coaching books.

My difficulty was that I was good and so expected to do well. How I envied those in the team who just played for fun – quite carefree and not burdened by any expectation of success. Somehow the expectation of that success made the pain of failure so much greater. I sometimes wonder whether teachers are aware of the damage they do by putting those talented at sport on a pedestal in a way which shifts the emphasis away from the rest of the curriculum. Young people deserve better than that.

"Dear bat," I would say to my friend and ally as I lovingly rubbed my hand over the blade while we sat together in the airing cupboard. That was how each conversation started, and from there our close relationship developed. At the time this unusual friendship was the most important thing in the world for a fanatical ten-year-old with a passionate love for cricket. When I now look back on those episodes, it makes me wonder how I could have behaved so strangely, and yet at the time it seemed the most natural thing to do. It certainly showed an abnormal amount of commitment for one so young.

My behaviour in the cupboard was odd; there is no doubt about that. Quite simply, it was important for me to discuss each match with my bat without being bothered by my friends. Indeed, had they known, they might not have remained friends for very long. It was, if you like, a tactics talk. Together we discussed all the shots we would try to play and how we would score our runs. It was a close partnership between bat and batsman. I knew I couldn't do without it.

Surprisingly, I was never discovered in the airing cupboard. My cover was never blown, and for nearly two years this procedure would dominate break time on match days. My unsettled and distracted appearance back in the classroom was considered neither unusual nor out of the ordinary. I had become very good at disappearing and then reappearing without incurring the slightest suspicion or even a raised eyebrow. Meditation in the airing cupboard was a strange pastime for a little boy, but it did help me to overcome some of the fear and insecurity that accompanies talent.

In the pages which follow, the airing cupboard is left well behind and becomes but a distant memory. And yet, as I developed and played the game in a grown-up world, there was always the little boy inside me, alone with the burden of expectation as he faced fresh challenges.

Echoes of that childhood can be heard below the surface of the pieces that follow, and perhaps those echoes add something to the tales.

I hope you enjoy them.

2

FAMILY

To what extent family ancestry influences future events is never plain but, on my mother's side, there was indisputable cricketing and sporting pedigree. Her mother was the product of a late Victorian athletic and, to some extent, intellectual dynasty whose influence and fame became widespread. The Ford family – my granny was a niece – were renowned for sport, music, art, education and the church. They were short neither of talent nor self-confidence. F.G.J. (Uncle Francis) played cricket for Middlesex and England, touring Australia under W.G. Grace's leadership. W.J. (Uncle Walter) for many years opened the batting for Middlesex with considerable success. H.J. (Uncle Henry) became well-known as a pre-Raphaelite artist, perhaps most famous for his illustrations of Andrew Lang's fairy stories. L.T.J. (Uncle Lionel) was headmaster of Harrow and later Dean of York. The Fords, there were other children too, were an impressive family both in stature, a handsome group by all accounts, and ability, which they were never too shy to display. My grandmother inherited none of these sporting traits but became a fine linguist, which served her well all over the world after she married into the Foreign Service.

My grandfather, Jack Troutbeck, was a serious man and a clever one too. After attending Christ Church at Oxford he joined the Foreign Office where, war excepting, he made his career. As a wise, thoughtful and perceptive diplomat he travelled first to Constantinople in 1928 and then Addis Ababa in 1932. With their young family, my mother and her sister Mary, they spent three years in Rio de Janeiro before being posted to Prague in 1937. From there they had to escape when Hitler and the German armies invaded in 1939. My mother clearly remembers seeing Hitler in Prague Castle and watching him inspect his troops. These grim moments of history in the making were somehow made more poignant by the young German soldiers, barely eighteen years old, playing hopscotch in the park with the children, including my mother then aged nine. My mother, who showed much early promise as a pianist, had to say goodbye to her beloved Jewish piano teacher, Herr Schechter who, with his family, would have been hoarded off with thousands of others to concentration camps and almost certain death.

After the war my grandfather was posted to Cairo, and there my mother met my father who, as a young diplomat, was working as secretary to the Ambassador, Sir Ronald Campbell. Interestingly my father's immediate boss was Donald Maclean who was head of chancery at the embassy. My father and Maclean became good friends and travelled in to work together in my father's old Ford Prefect, so Maclean's subsequent defection to Russia in 1951 came as a huge shock to my father. My mother said that he returned home on the night he heard the news ashen-faced and very shaken. What a waste of all that work in Cairo which presumably fell straight into the hands of the Russians. Since then, my father has always said that he has never quite been able to trust anyone again, especially if they're nice. Not quite true, I think.

Back to my grandfather whose final posting was to Baghdad in 1951, as Ambassador. Although not nearly as dangerous as it is now, Baghdad was nonetheless right at the heart of middle-eastern politics and subterfuge. Based in the spectacular Ambassador's residence, a palace on the banks of the River Tigris, my grandparents enjoyed their final posting which provided them with a fitting end to their diplomatic lives before retiring to Horsham in West Sussex.

My grandfather certainly wasn't unenthusiastic about cricket and played quite a bit in his younger days but with no great pretensions to competence. His brother, my Uncle Lancelot, was in a similar vein though he did bowl slow left arm, usually wearing a trilby. He was a Londoner at heart although, after Oxford, taught for a while at Lancing College in Sussex where one of his more rebellious and cantankerous pupils was Evelyn Waugh. Uncle Lancelot then moved to Westminster School where he became something of a Mr Chips, teaching classics and a little French. He lived near Victoria Station in rooms filled to the brim with Victorian furniture and had a passion for music, especially J.S. Bach. It seemed that all the Troutbecks loved Bach's music, and I was introduced to it on the gramophone when quite young. I too came under his spell, and the first piece of music I remember hearing was his 2nd Brandenburg concerto. I quickly came to love the other five too and, despite having to endure the slow movements, the jollier parts became my best friends. We didn't have many long-playing records then.

I confess to having a great affection for Bach and later at prep school had two postcards in my new wallet, one of Jesus looking down sternly upon Peter who had just denied him thrice and the other of J.S. Bach. At that stage I think I worshipped them both in equal measure. Uncle Lancelot, every Easter, went with his great friend G.G. Williams to a performance of Bach's St Matthew Passion, first in the Albert Hall and later in the Festival Hall. This was something of a ritual, and in 1964 he invited me and my mother to join them. It was all very serious, no applause at the end, and I was handed by my uncle a copy of the score.

"What's this?" I said.

"It's the score," he replied. "Bach 120 for 5."

A joke, and he roared with laughter.

By the early 1960s televisions were beginning to invade the households of Great Britain. Both my grandfather and Uncle Lancelot vowed that they would never be persuaded to watch such a thing. In the flat where we lived above their house in Horsham we took the brave step and hired a set. With Test matches now being shown live on the B.B.C. it was not long before both Grandpa and Uncle Lancelot were sneaking upstairs to watch the snowy reception. Soon after, a television was installed downstairs so that they could watch the cricket, and *Panorama* too – but nothing much else.

Let's now return to my father, long before his visit to Cairo after the war. Cricket really wasn't a great feature in his life although, around the age of ten, on visits to Dover he would attend the county cricket festival there and at Folkestone too. But Canterbury was, of course, the only cricket week that really mattered, and here he would watch the great heroes of the day: Frank Woolley, Percy Chapman and Tich Freeman.

My father was born in 1919 to my old Granny Barclay at Westwood Ho in Devon. By all accounts she was quite a character, rather large and not unformidable – a touch of grandeur. She was 40 years old by then and had been married for 15 years so was a little startled to find herself expecting a child. Legend has it that the doctor rode on his horse over from Barnstaple and quickly diagnosed the happy news. On hearing it, old Granny simply replied, "My dear man, don't be so vulgar."

My father was, like me, sent to Summer Fields Preparatory School at Oxford and then to Eton College before going up to Magdalen College, Oxford in 1939. Not much work was done then during those few months of freedom. It was more a time for pleasure before the war swallowed everyone up. My father was in the rifle brigade and went off to join the 8th army in Africa's harsh and unforgiving desert. All went well for a while until his old nanny sent a fruit cake out, via the Cape of Good Hope, to Badia, the regiment's headquarters. So eager was my father to taste the contents of the square cake tin that he took a short cut home across the desert in his jeep, ran over a mine and was blown up. His driver took the brunt of the blast and was killed while my father suffered from shock, superficial shrapnel wounds and a little deafness. He was lucky. What happened to the cake, no one could recall.

My entry into the world was a cold one. My father was based in Bonn, West Germany, and in January 1954 there were blocks of ice flowing down the River Rhine outside our house. I am told that to keep me warm my arms were strapped to my side leaving me with little early opportunity to exercise and no chance at all to suck either thumb. It was a disappointing start but fortunately did not last long. Within two years we were based in Horsham where the very early beginnings of cricket in the garden got under way. It was more the searching for balls in the flower beds that I remember than the contest between bat and ball. I quickly learnt that the quality of patience went hand in hand with cricket, right from the start and then for evermore.

My enthusiasm for the game was interrupted in 1960 when my parents were posted to Beirut in the Lebanon, a country not noted for its cricketing culture. Here I attended with my younger sister Jane the British Community School, to which we travelled each day in a brown, battered mini-bus. We greeted the driver with a cheerful 'Marhabba' or 'Sabehel-keir' which meant 'greetings' and 'good morning' in Arabic before boarding the bus for school. Our Arabic never became much more extensive than that. It didn't need to. Most of the children were British, American or French although I must confess that we didn't mix too freely with the latter. The Americans were a bit rough, too, and would use the phrase 'quiddit' – quit it – frequently enough for me to realise it was not a term of endearment.

I always said I hated Beirut because it wasn't England and there was no cricket. I also objected to the slaughter of live chickens; they ran about headless in the street before death came to their rescue. The food was filthy, too, the water undrinkable, and I lived on Bird's custard. For all that, the sea was beautiful and I learnt to swim in it using our embassy beach hut for changing. It was often said of Beirut that you could be swimming in the sea in the morning and skiing in the

Cedars after lunch. Not impossible, I believe, but you would have to be very keen. We tended to opt for one or the other, picnics in the mountains or a trip to Baalbek being favourite destinations. It was the lizards that intrigued me most about Baalbek as they scuttled in and out of the cracks in the large blocks and pillars.

Back in the city, social life seemed to be conducted amidst a giddy whirl of diplomatic cocktail parties, my parents whizzing off somewhere almost every night. From time to time we had our own party, a great many people crammed into our fourth floor flat, some of whom I got to know by handing around the nibbles – quite exciting. Amongst our many guests would have been Kim Philby, the double agent, who must by then have been living on borrowed time. A man of enormous charm and intellect by all accounts, he had, by 1960, fooled just about everyone and was now relying upon his cover as a journalist for *The Economist*. A communist since his days at Cambridge, Philby as a master-spy became one of the deadliest traitors this country has ever known and yet, despite arousing many suspicions, was still floating about in the Middle East in the early sixties attending parties, drinking a lot and seemingly enjoying himself. In 1963 he was spirited away to Moscow and disappeared for good. I am told that, amongst the things he subsequently missed about England, were the county cricket scores which presumably reminded him of a life long gone. They would always hold a place in the heart of an Englishman.

Back home again and coming up to seven years old, life had taken an irreversible change of course. My parents' marriage had come to a halt in Beirut and, without my father at the helm, my mother and her three children had to fend for themselves back in Horsham, not in abject poverty but with few pennies to spare. Friends and family can only go so far in helping out.

Amidst a fair amount of loneliness and sadness, cricket began to take more of a hold. My grandfather loved to watch the game at Horsham, and we would often walk around the ground. I closely observed the players in action and was particularly fascinated by the stumps and bails set at each end of the pitch. I would strategically place myself around the boundary edge in the hope that a ball might be hit near enough for me to field or retrieve it and throw it back to the fielder. I would be left for hours patrolling the boundary while the rest of the family went for a walk. It was a strange obsession to have, but cricket is a very strange game.

There would be endless games of cricket in the garden at Horsham. "Oh please will you bowl at me," was the clamour. The family would be persuaded to play. Everybody batted, bowled and fielded – even my sister Jane who would disrobe while fielding, preferring to keep wicket entirely naked. A flock of geese lived over the fence nearby and, although protected by blackberry bushes, they were never safe from bombardment. My elder brother and I would search for balls amongst the prickles, easing the burden by eating blackberries as we combed the border. Six and out for a hit into the geese was a well understood regulation. The match would continue until tea was laid out under the tree: teacakes – buttered – cakes and biscuits. It was worth stopping for.

At about this time we moved from Horsham to Henfield, some ten miles further south, and from there I was sent to school on the edge of Brighton, St Michael's. Here I was taught by Sir. He taught every subject including cricket and football, and it was his enthusiasm that really got me going. Endless games in corridors there were and cricket on a real field every Tuesday and Thursday, the two days of the week that really meant something. Not that we were very successful. In the only match I remember, against St Peters nearby, we were all out for 4 of which I made 2. I was very proud. As a result I was awarded The Huntly Trophy as the most promising player, an unlikely honour for which there may have been limited competition.

Holidays by the sea in Cornwall further fuelled my appetite for the game. I would stand on the beach at Daymer Bay, staring longingly at cricket matches being played on the sand. I made it quite clear that I yearned to join in and, after a while, my hopeful presence became irresistible to the participants who would invite me to play. The combination of sand in the toes, the tide coming in and a bat at the ready to hit the ball is one which must have inspired thousands of young cricketers the world over and enriched them with the desire to succeed and excel.

By this stage my mother had risen to the surface as the leading light in my cricketing life. Not that she knew much about the game; she would be the first to admit that she didn't. But it was, of course, my mother who drove the car all over the South of England, washed my clothes – grass stains and all – and cooked the meals. In fact, an endless round of chores that kept the show on the road. What with all that, and having to cope with the trauma of success and failure, things that meant so much to me and yet so little to normal people, she would do anything for me. On one occasion, when playing in an under-10s match at Cowfold, I left my precious bat behind at home. It was hardly possible for a worse thing to happen. Despite receiving advice to the contrary, my mother drove back to our house in Brighton and retrieved this vital tool of battle.

Once we had moved to Brighton and my mother had remarried, cricket went on all the year round. During the Christmas holidays I spent most of my time in the old chalet at the county ground in Hove where there were two rather low nets – not easy to flight the ball in there. With solid wooden run-ups, splintery too, and coconut mats and feeble lighting, the conditions were not ideal. But little did I care. I knew nothing else. It was cricket, which for me meant batting for as long as I could find bowlers to bowl at me. Old Jim Parks, who in 1937 had scored 3000 runs and taken 100 wickets, was my coach while my friends, Peter Hayes and Nicky Wisdom, bowled at me for hours on end. Peter went on to win a blue at Cambridge while Nicky was for a while on the verge of playing county cricket before running a successful sports business in Haywards Heath. Every now and then his father, Norman, would turn up and bowl, but he was not as accurate as Nicky or Peter and so not central to the scheme of things. Undaunted by the freezing cold winter and snow of 1963, the local bus replaced my mother's red Austin 1100 as a means of transport and dropped me within walking distance of the ground. On one occasion I staggered along icy pavements, only to find that the chalet was locked up and dark. Disheartened and disappointed I threaded my way back to the bus stop; it took nearly two hours to get home.

When not actually playing cricket summer or winter, much of my time was spent with my great friend, Jonathan Hoare, with whom I played for hours on the floor at home, either a game called *Cricket at Lord's* or Subbuteo football which everyone played. Both games demanded a lot of concentration and skill and so kept us quiet for hours. One of the most talented games players I have ever encountered and with remarkable catching skills, was Jonathan's golden, almost white, labrador called Venus. She sharpened up our football skills and as a goalkeeper would have rivalled Gordon Banks for reflexes. It was her misfortune to be a dog. Had she been a human she would, I'm sure, have been destined for an Olympic medal in some discipline or other.

By 1963 I was nine and at boarding school in Oxford. The West Indies cricket team, who were touring England that year, had, with their flamboyant and thrilling style, done more than anything else to turn my head towards the game. I watched them play at Arundel Castle in April and saw Gary Sobers hitting sixes onto the banks and into the trees that surround the lovely ground. Wes Hall, Charlie Griffith, who was reputed to throw his bouncer and yorker, and Lance Gibbs were all romantic figures. There were others too: Conrad Hunte, Seymour Nurse, the brilliant Rohan Kanhai and the dashing Basil Butcher. They combined great style with, perhaps surprisingly, ruthless efficiency. They were led by an outstanding captain in Frank Worrell whose tactical and diplomatic skills charmed so many of those who came to watch. I saw them play on television in black and white and listened avidly to the commentary on the third programme where John Arlott, Brian Johnston, Rex Alston and Alan Gibson painted vivid pictures with their words. Those West Indians were another great inspiration for my love of the game.

With my mother

With Jonathan Hoare

The spell of those long stints in the airing cupboard was broken by a particularly traumatic event which happened during a match between my school, Summer Fields, and our rivals in Oxford, The Dragon School. It was an encounter which the masters of both schools took very, very seriously. In this needle match I had been batting for some time and had amassed a useful score when, with confidence brimming over, I advanced down the pitch to a very slow ball. I swung at it and missed. In my haste to return to my crease I slipped over and fell despairingly to the ground and could only watch from this horizontal position as the wicket-keeper gathered the ball and broke the stumps with a loud appeal.

This dismissal would not in itself have been quite so dreadful, had my execution not been completed at the hands of a Dragons girl. This was a deeply humiliating moment which in the mid sixties was not one to make a young boy proud. Soon after reaching the pavilion, my bat and I concluded that perhaps, on the evidence of the day's cricket, we had grown out of our warm routine and would now have to contemplate life beyond the airing cupboard.

3
HORRIS HILL v SUMMER FIELDS 1965

Perhaps the most important and dramatic event of each year at school was the annual football match between Summer Fields and Horris Hill, a similarly Spartan preparatory school near Newbury and our arch rivals. The fact that Horris Hill remained unbeaten at football almost every season took nothing away from our determination to reverse this trend. I don't think we had beaten them in living memory and certainly not since the war. Upon each encounter we fervently hoped it might be our year, yet past results suggested that rarely did we keep the opposition score below double figures and hardly ever did we score ourselves. I was the Summer Fields goalkeeper and very small for the task in hand. I was given this responsibility because I was good at catching .... when I could reach the ball. I would constantly challenge myself to touch the cross-bar which, on occasions, with a running jump I could achieve. But Horris Hill was renowned for its full size goals, 8 yards by 8 feet, and that was a completely different kettle of fish.

Our master in charge of football was a bald, bespectacled man called Harold Hartley who, despite being a committed socialist and much taken with Harold Wilson and his government, was well respected. A diabetic and inclined to fits of temper and loud shouting, he was also acutely pessimistic and consumed by a gloomy outlook which rarely lifted. In my geography report for the previous summer term he described my work as "outstandingly bad – my impression is that he has made very little effort." Not surprisingly, he did not think well of me.

The journey from Oxford to Newbury was considered to be a long one. 'The lads' in the team would always occupy the rear seats of the bus where they would play games, sing songs and generally show signs of enjoying themselves. I always stayed at the front where places were reserved for those who suffered from travel sickness.

We motored sedately down the A34 past Abingdon and through the narrow streets of Newbury, over the river Kennet, until we reached the bumpy drive which took us to Horris Hill and the unwelcoming sign that greeted us, 'Beware of Adders'. At this point Mr Hartley bellowed to the bus driver: "Stop the bus!" Obediently, he eased his vehicle to the side of the road and Harold Hartley, master-in-charge and football coach, stood in the centre aisle and, looking at us solemnly, raised his voice. "I want you to know that today you will be beaten by Horris Hill and beaten badly. Drive on, bus driver." That was it, the team talk, the morale-boosting words to inspire great things. Mr Hartley was a Port Vale supporter and so strongly influenced by the expectation of defeat. He was also a realist and in his kindly way did not want us to be too disappointed when the worst inevitably happened. He had the boys' feelings at heart.

The sun was shining. The whistle blew, and the match started. It wasn't long before the black-and-white shirts of Horris Hill began to dominate play. A surging phalanx of them bore down on me as I valiantly tried to defend the vast goal behind me. The opposition seemed so big and strong and quick. Despite our best efforts we were no match for this ruthless onslaught. One, two and then three goals were conceded. After I had picked the ball up from the back of the net for the fourth time, I wondered whether perhaps as goalkeeper I would be better off wearing gloves. I had left my Peter Bonetti green pair neatly folded at the side of the goal and had been told by Mr Hartley only to wear them if it started to rain, which it hadn't, but for all that my hands were cold. It was a further worry to add to the sorrows of this match. If I could just get my hands on the ball to test out the merits of gloves. But it was not to be, two more goals flashed past me whereupon the whistle blew for half-time. A merciful release from this ghastly battle.

On to the field strode Mr Hartley, accompanied by a small boy carrying a large plate of oranges. Following behind them, rather surprisingly, was the bus driver. In those days a segment of orange was the standard half-time refreshment although for me, the goalkeeper, a cup of hot tea would have been preferable. As we chucked away our oranges, discreetly spitting out the pips, Mr Hartley critically dissected our first-half performance. My geography report came to mind as the words "outstandingly bad" were used to sum up our efforts. At this point the bus driver weighed in with a few words of advice. He was an Oxford United supporter and talked about "running off the ball" and "creating your own space". Mr Hartley clearly didn't like this rivalry for our attention and, had not the whistle blown for the second half, there could have been an embarrassing scene. The combined weight of Port Vale and Oxford United was not obviously helping the Summer Fields cause. These were, I presumed, problems that neither Bill Shankly nor Tommy Docherty had to contend with at Liverpool or Chelsea.

I wasn't much bothered with either the bus driver or Mr Hartley as I trudged off to defend the goal at the other end of the field. My mind was consumed with the horrid thought of having to endure another half hour of this grisly football match. As I turned to face the play, I was at once aware of a further problem which I immediately knew was not going to increase my chances of success. The sun had lowered itself just enough in the west and at such an angle so as to shine straight into my eyes as I faced the onslaught. Never mind the gloves now, where was my cap? I couldn't see a thing.

For a short while we staved off the threat of attack. But then it happened. The ball was kicked forward from the half-way line into my penalty area. I ran out to retrieve it and gathered the ball safely into my arms. I then ran around my penalty area regularly bouncing the ball (the law demanded this) pursued by the Horris Hill centre-forward. At last I felt ready to punt. I unleashed my kick, a feeble effort that was unlikely to relieve the pressure for long. It fell at the feet of an opponent who hacked at it in an ungainly manner. Meanwhile I was frenziedly back-peddling towards my goal. I saw the ball spiral up into the air … but then nothing, just the blinding rays of the evening sun and the knowledge that somewhere up there and coming in my direction was the ball.

Should I come out and catch it on the full or stay back and take it on the bounce? The opposition forwards were bearing down on me, big men they seemed with hairy legs. Standing by the penalty spot I heard the ball bounce. I jumped as high as I could but, sadly, never laid a finger on it and was unable to impede its progress onwards. It bounced inevitably into the goal. It wasn't so much the opposition celebration that hurt as the laughter. As I stumbled back to pick the ball out of the net, I saw Mr Hartley out of the corner of my eye banging his hand on his head and shouting, "My hat, that's bad!"

The sun sank lower in the west, and before too long the final whistle spared us any more agony. We had been beaten 12 – 0, a result which Mr Hartley, if not the bus driver, was fully expecting. While he, Mr Hartley, went off for tea in the comfort of the Headmaster's drawing room, we stumped off to have a much-needed shower. This involved undressing and baring one's immature body, both to the supervising under-matrons (very young) and the opposition. Normally neither of these two things would have mattered much. But what was very apparent to us was the enhanced maturity of many of the Horris Hill players compared to us. They were bigger and hairier, whereas we were still rather smooth. That, in essence, was the main difference between us and them.

Eventually, after tea, it was time to go home. Despite the defeat there would still be much singing in the back of the bus while, at the front, I would sit pondering over the events of the day and fervently hoping there would not have to be a sick stop on the journey back to Oxford. Mr Hartley also sat near the front, and several times on the journey home he muttered under his breath, "That was a very feeble performance." Given all the evidence, it was impossible to suggest otherwise.

4

ETON THROW IN A TIDDLER AT LORD'S

Lord's – was I really going to play on the most famous cricket ground in the world? Me, barely five feet tall, who, earlier in the summer, was playing in the Colts? 'Eton Throw in a Tiddler at Lord's', that was the headline in the *Evening Standard* and now here I was, sitting on the coach with a team of grown-ups (or so they seemed to me). They would never normally have bothered to speak to me but for cricket. Now we were part of the same team, on our way to Lord's to play against Harrow in the oldest and, for some still, the most famous fixture played there each year.

Wasn't fate an extraordinary thing? If I hadn't been hit on the foot in the nets back in May, I might never have attempted to bowl off-spin at all. Then, even if I had, I am not sure that many captains would have had the nerve to give me a bowl in the first Colts match of the season. But I made full use of the privilege of captaincy and brought myself on to bowl first change and to everybody's surprise took six wickets, never suspecting that the Eton captain was searching for a spin-bowler and had his spies out. He must have been desperate because, despite my age – just 14½ – and size, I was given a chance and soon found that older batsmen, too, could be fooled by slow, flighted deliveries.

We were now approaching London. I had only once been to Lord's before on the occasion of Sussex's great triumph in the first Gillette Cup final five years earlier in 1963. I had vivid memories of sitting on the grass in front of the Nursery stands with my godfather and elder brother, by far the best place from which to appreciate the mystery and splendour of the great Pavilion and watch the heads of incoming batsmen bobbing between members in the Long Room before bravely descending the steps on to the field. I remembered the crowd's excited hush as we awaited Dexter's arrival: silence erupted into a wild ovation as he strode imperiously on to the ground. Ten minutes later a chill passed through the Sussex supporters when Gifford had him caught at slip for only 3. For me this was the ultimate catastrophe, and I was convinced that Sussex could not possibly recover from such a devastating blow. A total of 168 was surely not enough, but the Worcester batting was gradually worn down by some relentlessly accurate Sussex bowling. Rain began to fall quite heavily, but nobody moved. Dexter at one stage placed every fielder on the boundary until finally, in the penultimate over and amidst ecstatic excitement, Bob Carter, Worcestershire's last batsman, was run out and Sussex had won by 14 runs to make my day complete.

I observed from the coach window that the street signs had NW8 on them so I knew we must be getting near and, before my mind had time to wander again, the coach swept into the ground. We were there.

With aching right arm I dragged my cricket bag into the pavilion, which consisted of vast staircases and long corridors all smelling slightly of rubber. Bumping my way along, eventually I found the home team dressing room which for some reason was allocated to Eton. The room was enormous but I spotted a quiet corner, dumped my bag down and collapsed exhausted on to a chair. Already I seemed to have walked miles and couldn't imagine how I would ever find my way from the dressing room to the wicket. As I looked round my eyes fell upon several cricket cases neatly stowed away under lockers: F.J. Titmus, P.H. Parfitt, W.E. Russell, J.T. Murray – heroes indeed! I had all their signatures in my autograph book, acquired after waiting for hours behind the pavilion at Hove. A favourite game was to trade autographs – a Titmus, a Parfitt, a Murray and two Russells for a Dexter, who was always the ultimate conquest. Now here I was, surrounded by names from my autograph book. I decided that I would sit next to Titmus's case as I knew he bowled off-spinners and hoped that some of his magic might rub off on me.

I must have been so immersed in the prospect of the match that I remember little of the immediate build-up, except that a huge wave of relief struck me when I heard that we had won the toss and elected to bat. At least I was spared instant activity and made the most of this respite by hungrily tucking into a splendid assortment of biscuits wheeled in on a huge trolley.

The match started, but within two overs my appetite deserted me; both opening batsmen were out for 0, and already I wondered when the number eleven batsman should pad up without affecting team morale. As it turned out I need not have worried because Faber and Cazalet, our most consistent batsmen, quickly repaired the damage with some fast scoring, adding 126 for the third wicket. But it was too good to last and, as soon as Coomaraswamy, Harrow's captain and left-arm spin-bowler, broke through, the collapse was swift. When Faber finally departed for a brilliant century I decided to prepare for batting.

Suitably protected I sat on the balcony, very silent, and surveyed the scene. There was a lot of noise and sporadic chanting from groups of rival supporters returning from sumptuous picnic lunches, whilst the cricket, oblivious to all this, remained intense. The atmosphere did nothing to soothe me as I waited anxiously for the ninth wicket to fall. Inevitably the moment came; Tomkin was batting, and very well too, when suddenly he chanced his arm once too often, rushed down the wicket, missed the ball and was stumped. With a lump in my throat I picked up my bat and gloves and hurried to the dressing-room door, so great was my concern to reach the wicket in good time. Down the giant staircase I went and into the Long Room, which seemed to be full of old men staring at me, and I wondered whether the crowd at the Nursery End would now be able to see my head bobbing up and down between the members as I made my way to the great door which led on to the field. Probably not, I thought; I was a bit small.

When I got outside it was very noisy. There was some abuse – 'Here comes the mascot' and 'They've reared him on gin' – but also words of encouragement, and I couldn't help remembering the Dexter ovation as I walked as fast as I dared to the middle, ignoring the cold stares of the opposition. At last I reached the crease and looked at the umpire. "Middle and leg, please," I tried to say, but no more than an inaudible squeak came out. "You've got centre there", the umpire answered kindly, which I acknowledged by banging the ground to mark my guard.

I looked around me and observed almost every fielder closing in intimidatingly and clearly not expecting me to last long. Meanwhile, Coomaraswamy was spinning the ball fiendishly from hand to hand, and I dared not look at him for fear of being mesmerized.

I took my stance. "Play," said the umpire, and Coomaraswamy trotted in and released the ball. As he did so, and without for one moment watching to see where the ball might be travelling, I thrust out my left leg and bat. There then followed the most joyous of sensations as, simultaneously, I heard and felt a heart-warming clonk as the ball by chance collided with my bat. Despite my paralytic fear I had now hit a ball at Lord's. "Over," said the umpire. I stepped away from the stumps and with great pride gazed up at the Grandstand scoreboard to confirm my score – 0 NOT OUT – and for a second or two I didn't feel anyone could ever have wished for more from life.

Andrew Douglas-Home, my partner at the other end, and I were determined to show that we could bat better than our positions in the order suggested. Sadly, the third ball of the next over was straight, Andrew missed it and we were all out for 210, Barclay 0 not out. What an achievement! I was so pleased both to hit one and remain undefeated. There may have been many more distinguished 0 not outs played at Lord's, but surely few that have meant so much. I strode off amidst great applause although I was well aware that it was not directed at me but for the Harrow captain whose marvellous bowling produced figures of seven for 42.

Harrow began their innings badly, losing an early wicket, and it wasn't until after tea that they settled down. It was then that I sensed I would soon be called upon to bowl. The summons duly came: 'Next over that end.' I tried to look confident but the only thing likely to spin was my head; would I ever pitch it, bowl it straight and spin it at the same time? Indeed, would I be able to release the ball at all? These were the horrors that began to overwhelm me while Douglas-Home bowled from the other end.

"Over," said the umpire at long last. There was no escape now; it was my turn. In the circumstances Kinkead-Weekes was the ideal captain, calm and quiet, and came to my rescue as I prepared to bowl. While I marked out my short run he spread the fielders out sympathetically, appreciating that I had to bowl at Webster, the Harrow opening batsman, who was already in full flow. "Play." I scuttled up to the wicket and hurriedly released the ball, a full toss on the leg stump. Webster's bat swung elegantly and cracked the ball past mid-on for four. How I got through that over I shall never know, but somehow I did and only conceded seven runs.

Slowly I found some rhythm, but so did the Harrow batsmen who, for a long time, were completely untroubled; until suddenly without warning, as the Grandstand shadows began to stretch across the ground, I bowled an innocent half-volley to Harrison, Webster's hard-hitting left-handed partner. He whacked it hard and low, and I turned to watch mid-on tumble to his left and cling on to a fine catch. A wicket at last, a wicket at Lord's; not my best ball but what did that matter?

It was nearing close of play now and, with Webster fast approaching his century, the ball was tossed to me to bowl the final over. The first five balls were played with the disciplined straight bat of a man determined to reach three figures the next day. "I'll try a swinger," I thought, as I walked back to bowl the last ball, and rubbed it vigorously on my flannels. The swinger was a ball I was learning to bowl as a variation from the off-break although I had not yet mastered the art of disguising it. Surely the mighty Webster was bound to spot it? Anyway, I bowled the ball and it began to drift gently away down the hill towards slip, enticing the cautious batsman forward to consider the tempting morsel. Webster continued to follow the ball as a salmon might a fly and against his better instinct went for it with a full flourish, expecting, I am sure, to end the day on a grand note. But it was not to be and, instead of a glorious stroke, the ball just nibbled the outside edge of his bat and flew to Cazalet at slip who snapped up the chance. Webster, caught Cazalet, bowled Barclay, 90. It was a wonderful way to end my first day's cricket at Lord's.

The following summer, 1969, Victor Cazalet was captain. He was the son of Sir Peter Cazalet, the racehorse trainer whose owners included Queen Elizabeth, the Queen Mother. Victor was a fine attacking batsman with a lightning quick eye for the ball. Not so comfortable with the quick single or indeed running between the wickets of any sort, he preferred to score his runs in boundaries and forego the mild indignity of too much exercise.

In 1969 the Cazalet family did the Eton and Harrow match in style. The old carriages were brought out of their sheds and displayed in all their majesty at the Nursery end of the ground.

Between them was laid out the most exotic lunch party imaginable for about a hundred guests including the Queen Mother and Elizabeth Taylor. I can't believe that either were particularly keen on cricket, but for me it made for a spectacular morning – huge long tables, white table cloths, silver, glasses, china plates and so on – it tested the concentration of even the most dedicated players. Between overs I tried to spot the celebrities on show.

The 1969 match was drawn, a result which seemed to keep everyone happy. In 1970 the match was played at Harrow, the first occasion in peace time since 1805 that this oldest of fixtures had been played away from Lord's. I was captain by this time, and we won with six minutes to spare.

Then, back at Lord's in 1971, my fourth appearance in the fixture, the match was once again drawn. I just might have scored a hundred in the first innings had Margaret Thatcher's son Mark – bowling innocuous off-breaks – not induced me to have a huge slog towards the short Tavern boundary. It was a bad moment for me to have my middle stump removed and then to have to contend with Thatcher's elaborate celebrations as I returned to the pavilion. "It was bad enough your missing your hundred," my friend Henry Wyndham said, back in the dressing room, "but, to give away your wicket to that chap of all people, that was truly awful."

Now back to the match in hand. The next morning Harrow continued to score freely, and it was not long before they passed our total. Naturally I was the target for much of this aggression, but the batsmen had to take risks in the process. I was lucky to be bowling still and had my captain to thank for maintaining faith in me despite the onslaught. Harrow were finally all out for 260, a lead of 50, and I finished with six for 100. For the first time in my life I was allowed to lead the team off the field.

Confronted with this deficit the match deteriorated quickly for Eton, and the two crucial blows came when Cazalet and Faber were dismissed in quick succession after lunch, Faber to a miraculous catch at backward short leg by Webster from a full-blooded hook and Cazalet lbw. We never recovered from this, and soon Coomaraswamy was bamboozling us again with his destructive spin.

In this second innings I was surprisingly promoted to number nine – a slight mystery; surely my 0 not out had not been that impressive? Once again I did not have to wait long before I was on my way down those stairs, through the Long Room and down the steps to see if I could improve upon my first innings.

The ground became very noisy, mainly with chanting Harrovians cheering their team on to victory. The challenge ahead was huge, but I was determined to keep my nerve. "Get forward, whatever you do, left leg down the wicket," Vic Cannings, the Eton coach, impressed upon me vigorously before I left the pavilion. Surrounded by blue-and-white-capped fielders I took guard, watched the ball (so I thought), and stepped back only to hear the ball fizz past me and strike the middle stump with a sickening clunk.

Out first ball, 122 for 8. Disaster.

I had had such high hopes of steering the team to safety but now, in an instant, these were dashed and amidst the uproar I was trudging, sad and lonely, with nowhere to hide, back to the pavilion. Why did I go back to it? I had meant to go forward. Yet another unsolved cricketing mystery. What would Vic say? Back in the dressing room it was very quiet, an atmosphere of hushed and uncomfortable tension with which I was to become most familiar in the years to come.

The match didn't last much longer, and finally we subsided for 141. Coomaraswamy was Harrow's hero, too good for us, and took five for 50 to give him match figures of 12 for 92. It left Harrow needing just 92 to win, which was achieved comfortably enough for the loss of only three wickets.

I knew full well that I might never play at Lord's again so, despite the disappointment, I found time to savour the extraordinary atmosphere before finally trotting up the pavilion steps.

5

CRICKET IS A LIFELINE

1969 was a good year. I was growing up a bit and, although still not very tall, was gradually becoming stronger and beginning to hit the ball to the boundary – occasionally. It seemed that all the coaching in the chalet at Hove was starting to pay off. Les Lenham, my coach, with broad grin and sunny face would from time to time proclaim, "Stop there. Hold it for a moment. Now that is the best cover drive I have ever seen. Ted Dexter himself could play it just as well, but he couldn't play it any better." Les would fill me with hope and confidence.

Alongside all this, my academic studies were going well too: 'O' levels, I got lots of them – including Maths, Physics and Chemistry. How pleasing it was to succeed in subjects for which one was wholly unsuited. For my 'A' levels I embarked upon the weighty subjects of History, Latin and German. I was expected to do well.

In July I played my first 2nd XI match for Sussex against Hampshire at Portsmouth. These were two-day games in those days, and I got a lift on the morning of the match from Hove to the United Services Ground with Alan Jones, our lean fast bowler. I think Alan would be the first to admit that he was then something of a wild character. Never before had I been driven with quite such carefree recklessness, and his pursuit of speed west-bound through Arundel's narrow streets made me wonder whether this was some sort of initiation ceremony.

A professional cricket dressing-room would have been an unsettling environment for most 15-year-old, public school-educated boys. But here I did have an advantage. Mostly the young pros knew me from my almost constant presence at the Hove ground, and some I could indeed count as friends and so share in the banter a little.

My first adversary on the field was Butch White, at the tail end of his career but still very hostile. A large man, a regular for Hampshire for many years, with a long run-up; I remember a lot of snorting and noise as he approached the crease to bowl. Not instinctively well-disposed towards a young public schoolboy he bowled with increased venom. At least I was well equipped with bat, gloves, box and pads though the absence of a thigh pad bothered me. My contribution was stout-hearted, determined but meagre, and I didn't even get to bowl either. This was the beginning of a long apprenticeship at Sussex, with much time passing between some very limited opportunities to impress.

In those days there was a lot of representative schools cricket – Public Schools, the English Schools Cricket Association and M.C.C. Schools. Early in August I was selected to play for M.C.C. Schools against Wilfred Isaacs' South Africans' XI in a one-day match at the Bank of England ground in Roehampton. A large crowd was not expected but, with play under way, I detected a gathering of students, long-haired and generally unkempt, on the boundary. At a given signal they ran onto the field, a pitch invasion, wielding placards denouncing South Africa and its racist policies. They sat on the pitch, Peter Hain and his friends, until dragged off by police. I observed all this from mid-wicket, having decided that a policy of indifference was best in the circumstances.

This mini-demonstration was a sign of how cricket was fast becoming wrapped up with world politics; it would be more than twenty years before South Africa shared the same international landscape with the rest of the world. Isolation played its part in ushering in a new dawn although at the time views differed widely on how best to achieve this end.

Then something happened out of the blue that was to have a profound effect upon my life and cricket. At school, as a result of my cricketing prowess, I had become a star pupil, glorified by the teachers and looked up to by the other boys – and not just those in my own year.

But for no good reason, towards the turn of the New Year in 1970, when I was almost sixteen, I began to lose the confidence and spark with which I was identified and to be consumed by serious and anxious periods of self-doubt. It was, of course, a dark time of the year, made worse for me by the lingering after-affects of influenza, which further lowered morale.

Towards the end of the Christmas holidays, my closest friend Jonathan Hoare and I invited – rather daringly, we thought – two girls for an evening out in Brighton. Fortunately they were both quite well known to us, which made life easier and also meant there was no real need for either of us to show off. It seemed to us that the evening, despite the cold and rain, had some potential. We took the bus into Brighton and there, at the A.B.C. cinema on the seafront, we bought tickets to watch *Butch Cassidy and the Sundance Kid.* The film, very popular at the time, was well received by all of us but particularly the girls, despite poor Robert Redford and Paul Newman coming under such heavy fire at the end.

We wandered out into the cool, damp night air and the sporadic burst of spray from the English Channel. Although I felt fragile and wanted to go home, duty compelled me in the circumstances to cross the road and take a closer look at the wild sea and foaming froth of the waves. This was what the others wanted.

Despite the wetting both from rain and spray there was for a while no enthusiasm to evade this onslaught of weather until eventually we relented and took refuge in a shelter facing out to sea. At this point I noticed that Jonathan had his arm around his girlfriend which suggested that, out of politeness, I should extend the same courtesy to mine. I got the feeling it was what was expected.

I confess that my mind was not on the job in hand when I plucked up the courage, leant across and bravely attempted an exploratory kiss. Considering the weather, and the damp and cold state of the shelter, my girlfriend showed a more receptive and romantic inclination than I had expected. This was in truth something of a blow because I could not at this crucial moment wrench my mind away from cricket. With a young girl looking up at me with some enthusiasm and even a glint in her eye, I was unable, I am ashamed to say, to think of anything else but the swing of my bat, this way and that, prior to making contact with the ball. It was a wretched predicament to be in and not entirely fair on her.

I think, looking back, I just about got away with it on the Brighton seafront that evening, but it soon became clear that my problems were far more serious than the after-effects of influenza. I was unable to get up and get going, I could not focus when I tried to read and it soon became apparent that I was suffering from a form of depression.

Depression is a foul intruder, I have found, and jumps out at you when it is least expected. It would be a long time before the depths of despair were finally cast off.

After a prolonged stay at home in the early spring of 1970, during which time I spoke to hardly anybody but my family, my mother and I travelled to Provence for a break, and I slowly began to come to terms with an illness that labelled me, in my own eyes, a complete failure. "He's hopeless, wet, can't cope." There are times in life when we beat ourselves up without reason. Depression – nervous eclipse, I have recently heard it called – is almost unparalleled in its vindictive and insidious nature.

So here I was, supposed to be something of a hero, showing great promise as a cricketer and academic and yet curled up in a crumpled heap of misery. I was deeply embarrassed that I no longer seemed able to function. Doctors came and went. I never felt they really understood the complicated nature of the problem. Depression or breakdown still remains a mystery, a chemical imbalance for sure, but oh so hard to treat. These days it is more talked about than ever before, but on balance I have found that anti-depressant pills have worked better than wise counsel. Despite adding to the confusion at times and occasionally sending you off to sleep unexpectedly, pills do lift the mood after weeks of perseverance. The main effect they had on me in the early days was that I never again bothered about academic work and exams. Instead, I just floated along, indifferent and carefree. A disappointment I must have been to my tutors – another Oxbridge candidate slipped the net, they may have thought. But no league tables then to worry about. It was the shame that hurt the most; that was the most penetrating part of the illness.

My recovery in 1970 manifested itself in an even more single-minded approach to cricket. I spent hours discussing the game with Vic Cannings, Eton's cricket professional, in his shop, *The Bat Shop* in the High Street. He took my cricket seriously and, more than anyone else, he made me feel better.

Vic was a wonderful man – and had been successful too in his own career as a fast bowler for Warwickshire and Hampshire. Together we plotted the new season, discussed tactics and arranged the programme, much as I was to do with Sussex ten years later. It all paid off. Eton's season in 1970 was outstandingly successful.

Vic teased us all relentlessly, and never did he let our feet leave the ground. My field placing, he said, was like confetti – throw it up in the air and the fielders were placed wherever it fell.

We defeated our main rivals, Winchester and Harrow, and I scored 897 runs which set a new school record. It has yet to be beaten.

After those awful days of January and February the year picked up. I was still taking the pills, and I became less affected by episodes of anxiety. By mid-July and the summer holidays I was rarely found away from a cricket ground: a mixture of Sussex 2nd XI cricket and representative schools matches. In one of these, played at Lord's, the Public Schools against the English Schools, I was fretting about a sore leg as we practised in the nets prior to the game. Charles Rowe, who was captain of the Public Schools, dismissed this as nonsense, which indeed it was; it highlighted for me the impact of nerves upon judgment before performance. As it transpired, I settled into an important spell of bowling from the pavilion end and, one by one, claimed all nine wickets to fall, including three who were to become close friends in the future: Geoff Miller, David Bairstow and Grahame Clinton.

I was perched on the threshold of taking all ten wickets in an innings at Lord's, but tea was approaching. I was given two overs to capture the final wicket, then the opposing captain drew himself up on the balcony, clapped his hands and declared. I had missed my chance, but I claimed some notoriety nonetheless.

Back at Hove with Sussex I continued to play in the 2nd XI. Despite the honour of playing in those matches and rubbing shoulders with the famous, I never got the chance to bowl even an over, and my opportunities for a bat weren't much better either. For some weeks I played a lot of cricket without actually doing anything. It seemed you had to wait your turn amidst professionals who, with understandable jealousy, guarded their positions with pride.

My lamentable track record, which must have been obvious to all, did not deter the club from selecting me to play against Jamaica in August, a match that had first-class status. I was what might be termed a late call-up. I was busy practising in the nets when at 11.15 a.m., fifteen minutes before the start, Mike Griffith, the Sussex captain, told me I was playing. I scarcely had time to panic and, gathering together my belongings, I hurried along to the home dressing room where all was quiet. We were fielding first. With the season nearing its end, we did not have a strong side and the expectation of failure hung gloomily in the air. It was a culture that did not lift for the next six years, at which point a new spirit of optimism mercifully changed the atmosphere.

There was little plan or structure to the cricket then, merely a drifting from one event to another in a contractual obligation which fulfilled the fixture list. I was too young to be disheartened or understand what was going on – and I was even given a bowl too. Although my opponents consisted of such seasoned players as Maurice Foster and Easton McMorris, I fared quite well. I nearly took the wicket of Foster, twice, but both chances – not tricky – got away, and I finished with nought for 56 in 17 overs. Then, as Sussex were twice bowled out cheaply, to suffer an innings defeat, I made 4 and 0. It was a match of no importance to anyone, it would seem, save for me – for I had now been launched into a new world of first-class cricket.

At the end of the match, I was seated upon a splintery bench in a corner of the dressing room, with the contents of my cricket case strewn all about me, when I was stunned to learn that I had been included in the team to play the following day against Glamorgan, the current county champions.

"We need to take a spinner to Swansea," was the explanation – a sandy pitch, apparently, that was conducive to slow bowling. Sussex were a bit thin in that department which was the reason why I, despite being only sixteen years old, was chosen to make my county championship debut. I was the only option.

I was not in the least bit disheartened by this; indeed quite the opposite, I was very excited. I discovered that I would be making the journey with two veterans of Sussex cricket: Ken Suttle, who held the record for the number of consecutive first-class matches played, and George Washer, the scorer. George had a weak bladder, and so was accompanied on the journey by a milk bottle which he filled from time to time before depositing the contents unceremoniously out of the window. Drivers following us may have been a bit startled and often had to use their windscreen-wipers. I confess I was taken aback by this procedure, but it did at least save time and

Ken, who always travelled with George, took it in his stride. No harm was done as we hurried on our way to Swansea via Bristol.

Whether or not Bristol was the most direct route in 1970 was not plain, but not for anyone were Ken and George going to miss the early season encounter between Bristol Rovers and Brighton and Hove Albion. Bristol won 1 – 0. It was a poor match; on this showing it seemed unlikely that either Bristol or Brighton would be challenging for promotion from the third division. Still, it passed the time and by nine-thirty, in the dark now, we continued our long journey to Swansea.

It was late when we arrived at our hotel, which was situated on a hill above the city in a thick mist. The tired night porter gave me a key and told me I was sharing a room with Michael Buss. I crept upstairs and unlocked the door. It was pitch dark and my room-mate was, from the noises he was making, clearly asleep. I didn't dare unpack for fear of waking him up; I slipped under the bedclothes partially clothed and lay there, worrying about what lay ahead.

Although I was very keen to play, it didn't come as a total disappointment when in the morning I swept back the curtains and saw that Swansea was engulfed in a thick drizzle which persisted long enough to delay the start. This did at least give me a chance to capture the atmosphere of a cricket ground in the rain. The bar was clearly the place to be and was filled with old men in mackintoshes having an early pint and discussing the weather. The players, in the main, retreated to the dressing rooms where they hoped to remain for the day. Most professionals fancied a day off when rain was in the air.

It was late morning when the covers were finally wheeled off and play got under way. Sussex batted first so I anticipated a long wait before encountering any action. Had I been more experienced I would have known that, even when batting at number ten for Sussex, there is seldom time to relax. True to form, wickets fell at quite regular intervals.

At the fall of the fifth wicket I slipped out of the players' viewing area and battled my way through the noisy and crowded bar to the steep stairs which led down to the dressing room where my equipment lay ready for action. Before padding up, a visit to the lavatory was imperative – the first of many – and just as important as the occasion itself. By and large, dressing rooms can be judged by the quality and quantity of their loos. The loo at Swansea was uncomfortable with paper like stale bread and not enough of it. Another wicket fell while I was getting ready, and I was joined by a disgruntled batsman who referred to the umpiring in unflattering terms. At least I had company, but I began to feel sick all the same.

At the fall of the eighth wicket I jumped up from my seat like a jack-in-a-box and fought my way through a throng of noisy Welsh supporters. "See you in a minute" and "Don't be long", one or two shouted as I began to descend the long flight of steps which would lead me onto the field of play. By now, with all the Glamorgan fielders staring at me, my composure and routine for handling tension had completely gone out of the window and I was in a blind panic.

"Middle and leg please," I said to the umpire and carefully marked my guard. The fielders were clustered around tightly, hemming me in like predators going for the kill. It was a frightening baptism. As if things weren't bad enough Eifion Jones, the wicket keeper, began to talk loudly in Welsh to the surrounding fielders, an unnerving tactic which completely put the wind up me, as was doubtless the intention. Malcolm Nash, left-arm over the wicket, prepared to bowl. He hadn't seemed all that fast when I was watching earlier, but now the ordeal was terrifying. He ran in unathletically and fizzed the first ball down the leg side harmlessly enough. I had at least survived one ball and felt reassured and marginally more confident. The second ball, though, was of fuller length and swung back at me late as I pushed forward. It struck me on the pad and was greeted by a huge appeal. The umpire, Hugo Yarnold, raised his finger unsympathetically, and my first championship innings was over. I had yet to hit a ball.

Not long after this the drizzle returned, and the weather set in to such an extent that the rest of the first day and much of the second was lost. The match wasn't able to recommence properly until the final day when much time had to be made up. A series of declarations was decided upon and suitable agreements reached between the two captains, Jim Parks and Tony Lewis. The long and short of it was that Glamorgan were asked to score 154 runs to win in about two and a half hours on a wet wicket. A run a minute was felt to be not unreasonable in those days, and Glamorgan had indeed struggled in the short time they had batted in their first innings. I was clearly expected to play a role in the Sussex bowling attack.

Unfortunately for Sussex things didn't go to plan. Bryan Davis and Peter Walker got Glamorgan off to a tremendous start and were determined not to be intimidated by any terrors the pitch might hold. It was during this onslaught that Walker hoisted a ball from Snow high over my head at mid-on and set off for runs. I turned and, in my attempt to make the catch, slipped and pulled a muscle in the top of my leg.

It was more the embarrassment than the pain which hurt me. I certainly couldn't bowl now, which was the whole point of my being in Swansea, and it would be hard to hide me in the field during a run chase. We had no twelfth man.

Things went from bad to worse. Walker, after a spirited innings, was replaced by Majid Khan who proceeded to carve his way elegantly through the Sussex bowling while I tried to remain inconspicuous and unnoticed. As luck would have it the ball chased me all round the soggy field. Glamorgan won the match at a canter by nine wickets. *Wisden* simply records that, "Possibly Parks was let down by his bowlers on a sporting pitch." It was an astute observation with which few could disagree.

But my day's work was by no means over. As the junior player in the side, in the absence of a twelfth man, it was my job to collect the tray of players' drinks from the bar and carry it to the dressing room at close of play. This was quite an obstacle course what with the crowded bar, steep stairs and the weight of hefty pints of beer and milk which the players had requested. I was doing quite well, had burrowed my way through the bar and successfully descended the staircase when, just upon entering the dressing room, I stumbled on a batting glove, which propelled me, out of control, through the door. For a short while I clung onto the tray brilliantly, balancing the drinks on top, but alas my luck ran out and I fell headlong, depositing the entire contents of the tray with a splash into Tony Greig's cricket case. As I watched items of Greig's equipment bobbing about in the smelly and unattractive mixture of beer and milk, I came to the conclusion that I must surely have played my first and last championship match.

It was two years before I played another match for Sussex, by which time I had recovered from the ordeal and was just about ready to have another go.

Only Greig remembered my clumsy introduction to first-class cricket. He couldn't rid his cricket case of the smell that permeated it, but shortly after my return to the team in 1972 he was picked for England and received a brand new case with his name on it. All was forgiven.

6

DUCKS GALORE

In 1972, at the age of eighteen, I became a professional cricketer. I suppose I must have signed a contract although I remember little about that, but I did get paid a small amount which was a step forward. Aware of making my first strides towards independence and also stealing a march on most of my friends who were either still at school or university bound, I was determined to take advantage of these new circumstances and wasted no opportunity to practise and train.

Hours were spent jogging over the South Downs in an attempt to improve my stamina and beef up my grit. Regular nets on the coconut matting back in the old chalet at Hove became part of the regime so as to prepare myself for the rigours ahead. For me pre-season started long before the seasoned professionals returned for duty.

At the end of each week, once cricket practice had started for real, I would collect my wages in a small brown envelope from the club's accountant and chief clerk who, like all of that species, was reluctant to part with revenue which, although only in his trust, he possessively regarded as his own. If he had only realised that the money was hardly my main concern at this early stage, maybe he would have replaced it amongst the club funds.

Despite having no form to go on, I was selected to play in the first match of the season at Hove against Essex – and I did well. Chosen primarily as a bowler, I didn't bowl at all – but, batting low in the order, at number ten, I scored 25 runs and held off for a while the power and pace of Keith Boyce, by far the fastest bowler I had ever faced. John Lever bowled fast left-arm and, after he had inflicted a particularly bruising blow upon my hand, Brian 'Tonker' Taylor, the Essex captain and wicket-keeper, comforted me with some fatherly advice: "Young man, at this level you can't wear gloves like that, get some new ones." It was like having an old friend out there in the middle with me. The gloves were thrown in the bin.

From this promising start, my game slipped quietly into decline. I neither scored runs nor took wickets. I also realised for the first time that I was playing for a poor side whose morale had for some years been going downhill. Apart from the occasional one-day flourish, expectations of success were low and I daresay the downward spiral had its effect on everyone. Whilst it may not have been a good time to play for Sussex, it did at least present the opportunity for selection and experience.

With that in mind, the Sussex coach, Les Lenham, approached me in early June and said, "Go and get some practice against Cambridge." The words were spoken as if success could be taken for granted, but the reality proved rather different. The match began peacefully enough. Rain restricted play to just an hour before lunch on the first day, in which Sussex fielded while an undergraduate from Yorkshire called Philip Hodson achieved something of a record by batting through the whole session without scoring a single run. It was an admirable piece of concentration much enjoyed by me and a handful of spectators who happened to be walking through the ground at the time. But it did little to set the heart racing.

I wasn't introduced into the bowling attack until mid-afternoon, by which time a partnership between Majid Khan from Pakistan and Dudley Owen-Thomas from Surrey was beginning to flourish. The pitch was flat and easy-paced; the sun had come out and runs came easily. By now a number of spectators had gathered in the afternoon sunshine, and they included a couple who had brought a bottle of wine along with them. This was quietly consumed before they proceeded without embarrassment to show much more interest in each other than they did in the cricket or indeed the bottle. They were positioned on the boundary's edge in the deep square leg area when I came on to bowl. Their behaviour did not go unnoticed by the players who took it in turns to field on the boundary and take a closer look at the absorbed couple. Amidst all this fun and games the Sussex cricket deteriorated quickly, and Khan and Owen-Thomas helped themselves to runs in the evening sunshine. Life at Fenner's seemed good for all, including the courting couple but excepting the hapless bowlers. I only bowled one short spell of four overs before being discarded for the rest of the day. So much for getting some practice at Cambridge.

I had always been a worrier, and that evening it concerned me deeply that I had been unable to contain the Cambridge batsmen, albeit that they were of high pedigree. I considered my bowling action critically. "Was I doing it right?" I wondered. It was a big question for me and one which I put to my room mate, Paul Dunkels, later that evening when we were preparing for bed. Dunkels was a giant of a man, six feet ten inches tall, and a fast bowler. In fact he had no intention of becoming a first-class cricketer at all but was just playing a few matches prior to joining law school in the autumn. He was a reassuring counsellor to an eighteen-year-old who was passionately keen to make his mark in the game.

"It looks all right to me," he replied sleepily although, in truth, I don't think he was much interested.

I slept fitfully and awoke in the early hours of the morning, restlessly churning over in my mind the mechanics of my bowling action. I got out of bed as quietly as I could in the darkness and carefully paced out my run-up from the window to a cupboard at the other end of the room, whose door I opened to give me a little more space for my follow-through. I was three strides into my action when I collided with something solid, which propelled me forward and downwards and onto the floor in a heap.

"What on earth is going on?" shouted a much startled and grumpy Dunkels from his bed. "You could have broken my legs!" Indeed I could because, in my enthusiasm to get my full run-up into the width of the room, I had tripped over the tall fast bowler's legs which had been sticking out at the end of his bed. We were now both wide awake so the very least I thought I could do was to make us a cup of tea while we discussed the merits of bowling over or round the wicket. Dunkels later became a barrister, but I doubt he ever had a more troublesome client than his room mate that night.

The match at Cambridge was not entirely wasted. It took place over a weekend on the Sunday of which the Sussex team, minus Dunkels and me, had to travel to Headingley for a John Player Sunday League match against Yorkshire. So I had a whole Sunday off in Cambridge to worry about my bowling and find something to do as well. I went to a church service in St John's College chapel and, staring down the aisle to the altar, could not get my bowling action out of my mind. I was obsessed by the problem and prayed about it but received no immediate comfort from the Almighty.

On the way back from St John's to the hotel, however, I had a stroke of luck which was to brighten up the day. I bumped into an old girl friend. Not really a girl friend, she was a girl whom I knew vaguely, and we got talking. Possibly my prayers had been answered after all. I rather rashly suggested that we buy a picnic and take a punt down the river Cam. I had seen many students do this before on the river Cherwell at Oxford when I was at school there. It was quite the thing to do. In those days we used to bombard the moored punts with missiles to try to splash the courting couples.

It was a lovely day so we hired our punt and set off on a crooked journey downstream. Complete concentration was required to keep the ship on course. The whole expedition and dinner afterwards can only be described as a success.

"Had a good day?" Dunkels asked me when I returned to the hotel room later that evening. "Any luck with the bowling action?" "Yes," I replied. "I found a remedy. Went punting on the river with a girl and never thought about bowling once." "That's what I like to hear," said Dunkels, and he turned off the light.

Unfortunately I didn't bowl in the second innings and, when it came to my turn to bat, I got a duck. It was not the practice that Les Lenham had had in mind.

As the 1972 season continued, the shine that might have been associated with county cricket became progressively tarnished. I did not contribute greatly to the Sussex cause whose ambitions seemed to decline steadily as the season progressed. There were no obvious signs of winning a match. Amidst all this gloom, I still got paid and there was meal money and travelling expenses tossed into the envelope too. We were just as expensive in defeat as victory.

But I had been lucky; I had been selected to captain the England under-19 side to tour the West Indies during the last two months of the English cricket season and so was able to escape from this uncomfortable rut. First-class experience of any sort was looked on favourably by the selectors and my appearances for Sussex, despite lack of distinction, had not gone unnoticed.

Jack Ikin, Lancashire and England, and Alan Duff from Malvern College managed the tour which introduced us to all the main cricketing islands as well as Nevis, St Lucia and St Vincent. Graham Gooch was undeniably our classiest player and was then a true all-rounder – batsman, bowler and wicket-keeper. Geoff Miller and I did most of the bowling – off-spinners – and we held our own against the opposition but no more. Whatever else, it was a welcome and refreshing break from the unenthusiastic nature of county cricket back at home.

To a large extent we had to fend for ourselves in the Caribbean. We rarely stayed in hotels but were billeted out with the families of our opponents with whom we travelled to and from the grounds. In Guyana, our last port of call, I shared an apartment with Grahame Clinton (Kent and Surrey) and Geoff Miller. Georgetown, its capital, is set in a low-lying basin, much of it below sea-level, and so is not surprisingly a breeding ground for mosquitos. Our rooms were a haven for these horrid, whining, bloodsucking scavengers, so much so that Clinton and Miller rigged up a device filled with toxic repellent spray and squirted the contents haphazardly throughout the rooms. The poison worked quite quickly and the wretched insects fell obligingly from ceiling and walls while we coughed and spluttered.

My breathing was severely affected by the fumes; Brighton's clear air had not given me immunity from the powerful effects of the insecticide – unlike Miller and Clinton who had grown up in Chesterfield and Sidcup respectively. It was a bad do and a bad night. That we survived is testament to our resilience on a tour where we had to work things out for ourselves. It did us no harm.

We returned to England in early September, in time for me to read the end-of-season first-class averages. I had started the summer with that innings of 25 against Essex, but in six more visits to the wicket I had added only another 14 runs, and my 45 overs of bowling had brought me one wicket for 111.

That wicket, however, was rather special, not just because it was my first one. Glenn Turner of Worcestershire and New Zealand was the batsman, and he was hell-bent on acquiring a useful not-out score towards the end of the second innings of a match destined for a draw. His plans were thwarted, though, by an unexpectedly vicious off-spinner; he pushed forward at it, and it burrowed a route between his bat and front pad and rattled into the stumps. It was a great moment, inspiring Tony

Greig to walk over to me from slip and say, "You'll never bowl a better ball than that in your career." He was right.

After a winter spent in Hong Kong playing cricket and, when I wasn't, working for a firm of stockbrokers, I returned to England fit and enthusiastically determined to improve on my so far unimpressive introduction to first-class cricket.

Although I did my utmost during a cold April to impress the new Sussex captain, Tony Greig, it came as a huge surprise when I popped into the dressing-room prior to our opening fixture to find my name on the team sheet which was pinned up on the notice board. I had been selected to play in the first home match of the season against Kent at Hastings.

Quite why we were playing the fixture at Hastings so early in the year was a mystery. That the timing was unusual and not likely to inspire a great deal of interest mattered little to me, as I was simply overjoyed to be included in the team so unexpectedly.

During the pre-season period it did not take Greig long to inject some much-needed zest and purpose into the lack-lustre atmosphere at Hove. His energy and enthusiasm rubbed off on everyone, and it was with a spirit of hope that we approached the early matches. Greig had himself taken Sussex by storm in 1967 when on his championship debut against Lancashire he had scored 156 and rescued the team from a disastrous start. From that point onwards this gangly youngster from Queenstown in South Africa could do no wrong in the eyes of the Sussex members. His elevation to captaincy was a natural and popular progression. He had charisma and style and, as captain, had a way of making the young feel good. He did little to disguise his ambition for the future which, in the short term, required him to make his mark on domestic cricket both as a player and captain.

At Hastings Greig lost the toss and we fielded first on a cold, blustery seaside day when gulls, squawking hungrily, outnumbered the spectators who were all wrapped up warm, with flasks of tea and coffee to sustain them against the fresh sea breeze. This was the opening match of the county cricket season, and it was stubbornly refusing to give way to the forces of nature and common sense.

I ran about in the field as enthusiastically as I could and tried to keep warm, just in case I was called upon by Greig to bowl my slow off-spinners. He stood at second slip from where he marshalled the game and cut an imposing figure – six foot seven inches tall, blond hair, dashing too, a born leader. Sure enough, despite the green tinge in the pitch, he brought me on soon after Colin Cowdrey had joined his captain, Mike Denness, at the crease. I was being thrown in at the deep end. Surprisingly both players, whether out of sympathy or just plain good manners, treated my bowling with the utmost respect, and I was able to settle into a quiet spell during which even the circling gulls held their peace for a while.

Then, all of a sudden, an extraordinary thing happened. I bowled a ball to Cowdrey who had been batting with unhurried serenity. It was not an especially good ball, a half-volley in fact but straightish, which he clipped quite calmly and politely in the air straight to Greig at mid-wicket who caught it. Cowdrey turned immediately for the pavilion as soon as he realised his mistake. At lunch he came over to me and said, "Well bowled, John." It was the fact that he knew my name which made such a mark on me. Despite this setback for Kent, Denness batted on to make an elegant hundred before declaring at 282 for five.

Heavy overnight rain followed by sunshine on the second day made near-perfect conditions for Norman Graham and Derek Underwood to exploit on a pitch left open to soak up whatever was thrown at it. In this case it was so wet that we couldn't make a start until mid-afternoon. "It'll be a pudding," I heard the experts say. "Too wet to be lethal." But it took just two hours for Graham and Underwood to bowl us out for 67.

I watched these dismal events from the dressing room window while I practised my forward defensive shot under the eagle eye of John Spencer, our medium-pace bowler, who gave me some coaching. I did not have to wait long for my turn. Trembling a little at the knees I carefully watched

Underwood as he emerged from behind the umpire after his long run up and bowled me my first ball. I thrust out my left leg and played what I thought was a model defensive push, designed to quash all spin and movement. Alas the ball reared up spitefully from a good length, struck me painfully on the thumb and was neatly caught by Cowdrey, fielding with many others in the slips.

The press box at the time was more interested in the season's first invasion of play by a dog and the first of the summer's witticisms from umpire, Bill Alley. Alley, according to Richard Streeton in *The Times*, reckoned that there were more fielding changes made by the Kent captain "than that bloke Fischer makes all day on his chessboard."

Anyway, I was out first ball. So I had to trudge in silence back to the pavilion to be greeted by my coach, Spencer. "Now, we've got to think of a way to get you off your king pair," he said, laughing, and with the second day's play rapidly drawing to a close I had all night to dwell upon the grim reality of professional cricket. I went home that evening and practised shots in front of the mirror that might get me 'off the mark' the following day.

The Central Ground at Hastings is, as its name suggests, right in the middle of the town and only a short distance inland from the English Channel and the town's famous fishing village. It smells of sea and seaweed and all things damp, just enough moisture in the air, you would think, to keep the seam bowlers permanently interested, not dissimilar to Scarborough's famous ground where I remember the North Sea fog sweeping in and rendering the deep fielders invisible. Swansea's St Helen's Ground is probably only a seven iron from the waves when the tide is in. Indeed all these seaside grounds are said to be affected by the tides which draw the water in and out twice a day.

Interestingly, although not particularly relevant here, seaside resorts have rarely provided us with flourishing football clubs. People tend to visit them for fun rather than football. Blackpool, of course, had its golden era but the likes of Southend, Torquay and Swansea, Southport and Bournemouth have never yet come up to scratch and so they join clubs such as Brighton and Scarborough on the perimeter of footballing dreams where great days are few and far between.

Len Creese, a useful all-rounder for Hampshire in his day and a man steeped in the ways of turf and grass growing, was both caretaker and head groundsman at Hastings. He lived in a room at the side of the old ladies pavilion and from these modest quarters looked after the ground. In 1970 he sold me a Gray Nicolls cricket bat with 'sub-standard' printed on the back. Although there were one or two knots in the wood, this bat proved to be one of the best I've ever had. He oiled it for me, too. Despite Sussex's batting collapse, no one blamed the saturated pitch which was certainly far from sub-standard at the start of the match. With his bald head and pipe, yellowing moustache, dirty hands, broken finger nails and shabby clothes, his character did much to shape the Central Ground. Not for him the strict guidelines of the modern age which these days mainly serve to stifle the skills of the honest craftsman.

The thunderstorms overnight were again so violent that it looked as if I might be spared batting at all on the final day. The ground was flooded when we arrived; there were large pools of water all over the outfield. I was much encouraged and filled with hope. Unfortunately, as on the second day, the sun came out and, while the Sussex players drifted about in miserable groups hoping it would rain again or at least that the Hastings ground drainage would prove ineffective, the Kent team, assisted by the local fire brigade, rolled up their trousers and waded barefoot through the water, helping to disperse it and allow play to commence – which it did at four o'clock.

Wickets started to fall, and Spencer was soon throwing balls at me across the dressing room while I attempted to perfect my technique for wet conditions and Underwood's bowling.

How hard it is to describe just how lethal Underwood could be on a wet pitch. From the age of 18, when he first burst on the scene with his distinctive left-arm cutters and spinners, he became a handful for even the best of players. From his long run-up he would appear at the last moment from behind the umpire, releasing the ball with a long, bowling stride and more of a medium-pace action. I think it was the wrist that did the damage and produced the poison with which the ball would spit angrily from the pitch. He was no fun to bat against at all.

The score was 26 for six when I went out to bat. I walked limply out, took guard and eyed the fielders all clustered around me like hyenas waiting to pounce. The first ball I received from Underwood was a quicker one. I pushed out blindly and surprisingly middled the ball with some power and timing, only to see Luckhurst at leg slip stick out his left hand and field it brilliantly. Still, it was good to hit one and I was off my king pair.

The next ball was slower and more devilishly flighted. It landed on the pitch and spat venomously at me as I prodded forward. Once again it hit my poor bruised thumb from whence it travelled in a gentle arc to Cowdrey at second slip. Out for nought again. A pair. A very low moment.

It was 26 for seven, and I now had no option but to wend my way back to the pavilion where I expected to be greeted by grim silence. Instead, I opened the door to find Spencer wreathed in smiles with hand outstretched. "Congratulations," he said. "A very honourable first pair. Caught Cowdrey bowled Underwood twice. What could be more distinguished than that?"

Soon afterwards, we were all out for 54, with Underwood finishing with figures of eight wickets for nine.

My Sussex career was not going to plan. In my infrequent appearances, spread across four summers, I had played 12 innings, and eight of them had been ducks.

Just when I was beginning to think things could not get any worse, they almost did. Batting in the very next match at Southampton against Hampshire, with my score still on nought, I pushed firmly forward to a ball from Peter Sainsbury and watched it soar from my bat towards Richard Gilliat at mid-off. He was not the swiftest of movers, and the ball eluded his grasp and trickled away for a single. It was only one run but, for me at the time, it was a precious one.

Notwithstanding Greig's enthusiasm for the young and my determination to improve, I sensed that my days in the first team were numbered – and this despite a bowling performance against Oxford University in the Parks which for a short while I thought might save me. On a cold afternoon I took five for 28 in 13 overs, including the wicket of Imran Khan who was caught on the deep mid-wicket boundary.

I was dropped and spent the next two months learning about the finer points of county cricket in the 2nd XI. At last I had a real chance to bat and bowl and learn about the game away from the spotlight.

In August I was back in favour, selected to play against Derbyshire at Eastbourne. Still I made few runs, scoring 4 and 0. But at least I bowled a bit in both innings and captured five wickets in all, including Alan Hill, Ashley Harvey-Walker, Brian Bolus and Mike Page. Now I had made some sort of contribution.

Sussex were again near the foot of the championship table, and for the next match at Taunton it was decided that our regular number three batsman, Roger Prideaux, would be rested. At this stage of my career I had scored 67 runs at an average of 4.19 so it was an extraordinary turn of events when Tony Greig told me that I would be replacing Prideaux at number three in the order. It was a wholly unjustified vote of confidence but typical of Greig's approach to the game. He was always prepared to take a chance.

Elevated to this lofty position of responsibility, I was determined not to waste my opportunity when it arrived. We won the toss and batted first. As was so often the case with Sussex in those days, I did not have to wait long for my turn to bat and, when it came, I set out to occupy the crease for as long as possible against the hostile bowling of Alan Jones, Hallam Moseley and especially Tom Cartwright, the like of whom I had never come up against before. Cartwright never bowled a bad ball. He swung it both ways and cut the ball off the pitch. He wasn't exactly fast and indeed the wicket-keeper, Derek Taylor, stood up to him.

I was a bit disconcerted by Taylor who engaged me in polite conversation while I was trying to fathom out the mysteries of Cartwright. "Is it right," he asked me, "that your grandfather was Prime Minister?" I was somewhat taken aback by this enquiry while Cartwright was walking back to his mark. "No," I said. "You're thinking of Mark Faber who's coming in later."

The gentle banter continued throughout the morning. Perhaps Taylor was trying to put me off, disrupt my concentration or, more likely, he was bored and just trying to keep himself on the ball.

Despite all this I survived the initial onslaught and eventually, by way of variety, Brian Close, the Somerset captain, brought himself on to bowl his off-spinners. Close was for me one of the legendary figures of cricket. Recruited by Somerset from Yorkshire and with a reputation for being one of the game's hard men, he cut an imposing and intimidating figure with the ball in his hand. I could remember listening on the wireless to his epic innings against the West Indians in that famous Test match at Lord's in 1963 when his 70 runs on the last day, amidst a barrage of short bowling from Wes Hall, brought England to within a whisker of winning that extraordinary game. And here I was now, aged 19, being confronted by one of my heroes.

For some reason Close had decided to bowl his off-breaks around the wicket, and I immediately encountered a problem. It wasn't caused by the skill of Close's bowling but rather by my habit, after I had played each shot, of running down the pitch a few yards in the hope of stealing a much-needed run.

"You can't run straight down pitch like that, laddie," Close exclaimed. "Arthur," Close turned to the umpire, Arthur Fagg, for support. "Tell him to run off pitch." Taylor from behind the stumps joined in the debate. I felt outnumbered. Despite all my best efforts I kept on scampering down the pitch. "He'll have to change his shoes," said Fagg and went to consult his fellow umpire Tom Spencer, who looked a bit like Popeye under his white flat cap. "All this fuss about shoes," I muttered, "as if batting wasn't hard enough." I didn't have any other shoes, anyway. In the end we came to some sort of truce whereby

I stopped trying to take quick singles off Close. Run-scoring dried up almost completely, and the problem was ultimately solved when I clipped a ball from Close to mid-wicket where Rose caught it.

Nevertheless I had managed to make my turgid batting last four and a half hours, in the process scoring 52, my first first-class fifty.

The next day was not so glorious. Late in the Somerset innings I was fielding close in at short leg, as youngsters do, when Moseley clipped a ball fiercely off his toes, and it caught me a severe blow on the head. Unlike Close who would have stood there and shouted "Catch it," I collapsed to the ground in a heap and was carefully ushered from the field to the darkness of the dressing room where I nursed a severe headache. When it was Sussex's turn to bat again that evening, I was not well enough to go out

But the day was far from over. My cousins from Chewton Mendip, who had been watching, came round to the pavilion at close of play to enquire after my well-being and suggested to me that an evening's fishing might provide a peaceful remedy for my aching head. I readily agreed, and we set off to Litton Reservoir nestling in the Mendip Hills. Litton, reserved for the directors of Bristol Waterworks, was rarely fished and stocked generously with fat and fairly stupid rainbow trout. We could hardly fail.

Fishing, I find, is a peaceful cure for most things, and within two hours my headache had gone and three plump trout had been netted.

The next morning Somerset bowled Sussex out for 118 and won the match comfortably by seven wickets. I followed my first innings fifty with another duck.

As the game worked out, Close had had no need to be worried about my prolonged and irritating stay at the crease. "Get yourself some plimsolls, laddie," were his final words to me as we departed.

7

UNEXPECTED DEVELOPMENTS
IN THE WEST INDIES

The winter of 1973-74 was long and chill, and the full force of the miners' strike, the three-day week and the final days of Edward Heath's government combined to make life a misery for many. I was just nineteen years old and, although completely obsessed with cricket, was starting out on my first winter job as an insurance trainee based in the City of London. I began as a 'life and pensions' man, a fate for which I could tell at an early stage I was clearly unsuited.

My employers fervently hoped that I would introduce business to the company and sign up all my friends with life insurance and savings policies to safeguard their futures. In truth I was a bitter disappointment to them and, after three long winters during which the nation's economy appeared to slide to its lowest ebb, I think I sold one frail and unconvincing endowment policy, which doubtless in the end did not do what it was supposed to. That this dismal record bothered me so little should have been of some concern, but my mind was on other things.

What really did bother me was my progress in the world of cricket and particularly my training programme for the winter. You might well imagine that, back in those bleak, dark months all those years ago, there was little to be done with cricket. If so, you'd be wrong. Every Tuesday night I would slide off from work in the City a little early and drive across London to Alf Gover's famous cricket school in Wandsworth, a haven for a host of aspiring players, where Alf himself, tall and smart in white flannels, England sweater and white cravat, was entrusted with the task of teaching me how to bowl off-spin. This was quite a challenge for us both.

What triggered off this desire to spin the ball was a match played the previous August between Sussex and Middlesex on a surprisingly dry and dusty pitch at Hove, an ideal surface for spin bowlers to show their worth. For Middlesex, Titmus and Edmonds took full advantage of these helpful conditions and between them captured eighteen wickets in the match, reducing the Sussex batting to a gibbering and hesitant wreckage. Nobody mastered this formidable challenge to their technique, and consequently we lost the match by an innings and 182 runs.

In contrast to the successful Middlesex spin attack I failed to take a wicket despite lengthy spells of bowling. It was like fishing down a stretch of river full of trout without getting so much as a nibble for one's labours. I sat disconsolately in the dressing room at the conclusion of the match and listened to the senior players as they chewed over the remains by way of a post-mortem. "How come it only spins when they bowl?" someone asked. I felt awful and slouched lower into my corner. "John, you've got to learn to spin the ball." At this point several Middlesex players, drinks in their hands, entered the dressing room and joined in with the banter. Amongst them was the master of off-spin, Fred Titmus.

"Fred, what do you make of our young off-spinner?" he was asked. Titmus considered the question for a moment before nodding his head in conclusion. "Promising," he said encouragingly. "Very promising. But he needs to learn to spin the ball. Send him off to Alf Gover this winter. He's the man to do the trick."

So my destiny for the winter months was decided upon. The Alf Gover Cricket School in South London. It was the devil of a place to find on a cold dark evening, rain pouring down, windscreen wipers hissing and confronted by blinding headlights. The premises were carefully concealed behind a garage in what appeared to be a shabby old warehouse, dimly lit by gaslights. There I found a large, oldish man, whom I later discovered was the former Somerset player, Arthur Wellard, mending holes in the netting while another, Lofty Herman, lit the remaining gaslights with what looked like an old snooker cue. The floor seemed to consist of a series of rubber mats unevenly stacked on top of each other to produce an undulating surface on which to play. There wasn't much room for a bowler's run-up.

It was in these unpromising surroundings, that would have had today's health and safety officers shaking their heads in despair, that I embarked with my coach, Alf Gover, upon the magical world of spin. I enjoyed those sessions with Alf very much. He was so encouraging. "My dear boy," he would say, "we'll get you spinning the ball for sure." And gradually his coaching and enthusiasm had the desired effect. At least I could see the ball spin when it hit the mounds of matting, although I got the feeling that anyone would have been flattered by that surface.

"Shoulders and hips twisting," he would say, "and pivot round that front foot. My dear boy, that's coming on. Well done." I liked his style. "Alf will improve your bowling," Titmus had told me, and he was right.

Towards the end of the previous summer I had received a telephone call from Jim Swanton, the *Daily Telegraph* cricket correspondent. Amongst his many interests in life, and there were many, he founded and presided over his own cricket club which, many years earlier, had been named 'The Arabs'.

"We're going on a cricket tour to Barbados after Christmas," he boomed down the telephone. "I would like you to come. It will do you good. I trust you're not doing anything else then." I was thrilled, of course, to have been invited on such a prestigious tour, not that I could possibly have said no, even if I had wanted to. Swanton wasn't the sort of person you said 'no' to without very good reason, and his influence upon the game and its people was considerable. Essentially he was a kind man and, although even his greatest friends could not deny in him a hint of pomposity and grandeur, much of it, once you got to know him, was tongue in cheek and certainly not to be taken too seriously. A big man in every sense of the word, Jim's life had, more than anything else, been shaped by his experiences at the hands of the Japanese as a prisoner of war; they brought out in him traits of humility and affection not associated with a man who was scarcely lacking in confidence. It is true that Jim was quick off the mark when a Duke or Duchess came into view and royalty too did not often escape his attention but, for all that, he took trouble over ordinary people and would spend time in conversation with them and help wherever he could.

When we arrived in the Caribbean, it did not take me long to discover that this was no ordinary cricket tour. On my previous tours overseas with the England under-19 teams, we had often talked about cricket and tactics by way of passing the time in dressing rooms and on trains. In Barbados the balance of conversation could not have been more different. The discussion revolved around the stock market where turbulence and volatile conditions concentrated the minds of the players. The property market and something called secondary banking were not far behind. Both appeared to be in a state of collapse – I'm told that 'correction' is now the word – but this, from the long faces drawn, seemed to go further. In 1974 the British economy was facing dark times. The miners, and Arthur Scargill in particular, were both powerful and militant. Edward Heath called a February general election based on his question, "Who runs the country, the miners or the Government?" He quickly got his answer and was shunted aside in favour of Harold Wilson.

Aged 19, I had been thrust into a grown-up arena which reached out far beyond my narrow world of batting and bowling. Here we were in Barbados in the flamboyant world of the fast bowler and hard-hitting batsman, with rum punches round every corner.

Tony Lewis was the Arabs captain. He had for several years led Glamorgan with distinction and in 1972 captained M.C.C.'s England team in India and won the Test series there with all the odds stacked against visitors. Now on this tour in Barbados, Tony, although bolstering our experience and expertise, was recovering from knee operations – the wear and tear of rugby and cricket – which rendered him tentative on both legs.

Even in practice we were up against it. Tony, always with a sharp eye for an opportunity, was quick to recruit two of the waiters at the Coral Reef Hotel, where we were staying, to reinforce our bowlers at net practice. Little could he have known that they would bowl with such pace and bounce and so alarm the batsmen, pale-faced and naively hopeful after a winter spent in the office at home. It was a miracle that we emerged unscathed – apart from Richard Hutton, who damaged a finger but was not allowed to make a fuss because of his Yorkshire background. From then on, the waiters confined their activities to pouring drinks.

We were not long into the tour when we were subjected to a three-day match against a Barbados team at the Kensington Oval in Bridgetown. It was a great occasion because Gary Sobers came to watch for a while. He made up for the small attendance of spectators and, as everyone's ultimate cricketing hero, we would have been quite happy to fall victim to earthquake or pestilence then and there. He was Jim Swanton's greatest hero, too. I don't think even the Queen would have distracted him that morning.

The Arabs batted first. Opening the bowling for Barbados was a man of some stature and charisma, sporting a distinguished beard and called Gregory Armstrong. "He's a bit wild," Gary Sobers told us, and at first we thought – or at least hoped – that he was referring to parties and nightclubs. "He's the quickest in the world," he went on.

Up to then the fastest bowler I had faced had been Keith Boyce at Essex, and one of us suggested Boyce's name as somebody who might be quicker. "Boyce?" Gary replied. "Medium pacer."

Armstrong came in off a thirty-yard run-up, and he was clearly keen to impress both Bajan and West Indian selectors – and Gary Sobers too.

If my memory is right, Richard Hutton opened the batting with Stanley Metcalfe, another robust Yorkshireman and uncommonly brave too as it turned out. Metcalfe got firmly onto the front foot despite the pace and bounce: not for him to alter his well-established technique and lifetime of good habits. The result was that he took several blows to the head, protected only by his Oxford Harlequins cap, whence the balls shot off for runs in the fine leg direction. This was useful to the team because it got the scoreboard moving, but uncomfortable for Stanley. No permanent damage was done and, as years went by, he pursued a most successful business career in which ultimately he became chairman of Rank Hovis MacDougall where doubtless his exploits as an opening batsman became legendary.

Throughout the morning the Arab batsmen were traumatised by Armstrong whose excessive pace was enhanced by his long bowling stride which caused him to release the ball from closer to the batsmen than they would have wished. A no-ball is of little comfort to a batsman as it whistles past his nose on its way to the wicket-keeper. The Arab batting failed to master this onslaught in either innings. "Use your feet," Swanton bellowed from the boundary. From this advice it wasn't plain whether we should be treating Armstrong as one might a spinner and nipping down the pitch to disrupt the bowler's rhythm or, alternatively, making an unheroic run for it, presumably in the square-leg direction. Whatever we did, it amounted to the same thing: abject failure and humiliation. If we didn't actually lose by an innings, we jolly nearly did. The Founder (Jim Swanton) called for greater commitment, and he made it clear to us all that he looked unfavourably upon his team giving way with so little fight.

After several sessions with Alf Gover, I had arrived in Barbados full of hope for my bowling and in the first match, when the batsmen had all tried to hit me out of the ground, I had taken five wickets for only three runs. But after that things started to go downhill. The hard, true pitches on the island didn't seem to take the turn that Alf's undulating mats had done, and my bowling reached a low point in a match against a club called Spartan.

At lunch we had kept them to just 87 for two but after the break they added another 188 in only 80 minutes, with two Test cricketers, Peter Lashley and Collis King, hitting my bowling everywhere. According to the tour report in the *Cricketer* magazine, Lashley was 'virtually nominating branch and leaf off Barclay' while King, in the hot sunshine, hit the ball with extraordinary ferocity. At one point, shortly after I had released the ball, he ran down the wicket towards me and hit it back with such power, as I tried to retreat, that it ricocheted off the solid white wall of a sightscreen and arrived back at my feet like a boomerang.

Sorry as I was to see it back again, I prepared to bowl the next ball, fervently hoping that my reactions would be up to the mark. As I passed the umpire he turned to me and asked whether I would mind if he stood a little further back. "Not at all," I replied. "The safest place would probably be just behind the white wall." He did laugh, which is of course what cricket in the West Indies used to be all about. It was clear that I had a lot more work to do if I was to be the spin bowler Sussex wanted me to be.

Whilst the cricket performances on the field gradually went from bad to worse, off the field there was enough distraction behind the scenes to ensure that the tour for all its drama was neither wholly unsuccessful nor dull. Barbados is a beautiful island, encircled by stunning beaches and a sea so clear that colourful fish can be identified and pursued to the heart's content of a diver. Rum punches arrive with little prompting, ice clinking gently against the glass, and food too will appear as if by a conjurer's trick to satisfy the desires. It is a truly wonderful place.

Amidst this blissful world it had not gone entirely unnoticed that one of our players had not only brought his very beautiful wife to Barbados but also a far from unattractive nanny to look after their four-year-old son. It became apparent, as the tour went on and the cricket pursued its journey downhill, that nanny began to extend her range of services beyond those of looking after children.

Unexpectedly, towards the end of the tour and very much against my natural inclinations amidst cricket as important as this, I got the feeling that nanny, probably in her late twenties, had taken something of a shine to me, the teenager. Nannies had not been a part of my life in the past so this newfound attention was as welcome as it was improbable and against the run of play. In truth, it had to be admitted, I was something of a beginner and so rather naïve when it came to any attention from the opposite sex. But Barbados did seem to be as good a place as any to get going and with a woman of some experience – almost too good to be true. The quantity of sand surrounding the island might have been seen as a drawback, but on the whole I found I was in no mood to grumble about that. I just couldn't believe my luck.

The fact that I may well have been batting lowish in the order might for some have been considered a disadvantage, but this did not deter me one bit. In fact I thought it was quite flattering to follow a pretty distinguished list of cricketers. Be that as it may, nanny did a great deal to lift the morale of such a challenging tour. I think even Jim was surprised at the tenacity of his players and their ability to keep going in troubled times.

The outcome of these shenanigans could not have been more satisfactory and, with minds briefly diverted from the discomfort of facing up to so many talented West Indian cricketers, we began to perform better on the cricketing front too. It all goes to show that women on tour sometimes have an important part to play and that success is often rooted in what goes on behind the scenes when the curtain comes down.

I imagine that Jim never quite knew the full story, indeed he didn't need to. Endearingly he attributed our unexpected improvement to some conscientious practice under the watchful eye of Tony Lewis. For all that, he was a journalist at heart, albeit rather a grand one; he had an inquiring mind and a sense of fun too. "Well done and well played," he said to us after our final match when the Arabs were victorious at last. "That's better." With that and with a knowing look in his eye, he raised his eyebrows a little and smiled with a broad grin, mouth clamped shut and no teeth to be seen. On that note the tour ended.

As we left Barbados, we were replaced on the island by the MCC, captained by Mike Denness and starting out on a three-month tour of the West Indies which would take in five Test matches. To underline the chasm between our cricket and theirs, they opened their first game – against the President's XI – by scoring 511 for four, with our scourge Gregory Armstrong taking nought for 106.

Back as an insurance trainee in the City of London I would journey after work to the Middlesex Cricket School at Finchley where Don Bennett, the head coach, allowed me to join in and practise with the Middlesex players. Here I tried out my spin bowling assiduously with Edmonds and Emburey, who were always there and showed me the way.

On one of those evenings, when we were chatting in the bar after a vigorous session in the nets, the topic uppermost in our minds was the latest Test match between England and the West Indies in Port of Spain. All the talk was about Tony Greig who, highly controversially, had just run out Alvin Kallicharran off the last ball of the second day's play. You may remember the incident. Underwood bowled to Bernard Julien who pushed the ball a yard or two past Greig fielding very close, all six foot seven inches of him, at silly point. Greig quickly turned to retrieve the ball while Knott, the wicket-keeper, pulled up the stumps for close of play and Julien turned for the pavilion behind him. Kallicharran, the non-striker, backing up as usual, merely continued his walk towards the dressing-rooms as he removed his gloves. Greig, meanwhile, aware that Kallicharran had strayed out of his ground, picked up the ball and hurled it ferociously at the bowler's stumps while Underwood was retrieving his sweater from the umpire, Dougie Sang Hue. Greig's swift action took everybody by surprise and scored a direct hit on the stumps which were dramatically shattered, much to Underwood's relief – he would have hated to have conceded four overthrows off the last ball of the day. Wildly enthusiastic as always, Greig appealed and Sang Hue was left with no option but to give Kallicharran run out. All hell was then let loose in the pavilion. There were angry crowd scenes all around the ground while officials of both camps barricaded themselves into the dressing-rooms for more than two hours before issuing a statement saying that "in the interests of cricket generally and the tour in particular the appeal had been withdrawn and Kallicharran would resume his innings in the morning."

"Shame," concluded the young players in the bar at Finchley, especially after watching the incident on a news programme. We were all on Greig's side and felt Kallicharran had been careless and presumptuous. Kallicharran went on to score 158, and West Indies won the match comfortably by seven wickets. That was the first Test match in the series. In the last, also at Port of Spain, the tables were dramatically turned and once again it was Greig who played the leading role, this time with the ball. He had foregone his usual medium pace and taken up off-spinners instead, and these he bowled at good pace from his considerable height.

Perhaps encouraged by the number of left-handers in the West Indies team, Greig extracted bounce and turn that not even his fellow spinners – Underwood, Pocock and Birkenshaw – could manage. Greig took thirteen wickets in the match, and I was left feeling a little disheartened. Despite all Alf Gover's coaching and well-meaning spirit and the hours spent at Finchley too, it seemed to me that out in the Caribbean Sussex had at last discovered someone who really could spin the ball as much as Titmus and Edmonds. Sadly it wasn't me.

8

SUSSEX AT ITS LOWEST EBB

Ever since those heady days in the early sixties when Sussex twice won the Gillette Cup under Ted Dexter's leadership, the new concept of one-day cricket was deemed to have its roots in Sussex. For some while we were considered to be the one-day specialists.

But it did not take long for those early days of success to be replaced by disappointment and, occasionally, despair. Three times between 1968 and 1973 Sussex reached the final, only to be defeated each time – by Warwickshire, Lancashire and Gloucestershire. Sussex had lost the knack of winning – or perhaps the opposition had caught us up with their own formula.

By 1975 little had happened to improve the plight of Sussex cricket. Greig was now captain of England and had his mind on loftier matters. The young players were not progressing as they should; indeed, if I glance at my own figures for 1974 and 1975, it is astonishing I was selected so often. I was still in the "promising" category but only just.

We were bumping along at the bottom of the county championship and had already been knocked out of the Benson & Hedges Cup at the qualifying stage when we visited Nottinghamshire at Trent Bridge for the Gillette Cup first round on a fine day at the end of June. For a while all went well for Sussex. Tony Greig won the toss and, after electing to field, watched to his delight the opposition subside to 117 for eight, a score made worse for Nottinghamshire by an injury to Peter Johnson, their middle-order batsman, who had to leave the field after being felled by a John Snow bouncer.

But a bit of blood on the pitch seemed to inspire the Nottingham tail. Bill Taylor had never batted higher than number eleven before but, once entrusted with some responsibility, he relished the challenge. At the time he was probably the worst batsman I had ever seen. He stepped away from his stumps and flayed wildly with his bat. It was remarkable that he hit the ball at all, yet he struck it all over the field and mostly to unexpected places where there weren't any fielders. Greig lost his temper and 'Wild Bill' flourished to such an extent that, by the time he finally got out, Johnson was back from hospital and able to add to the mayhem himself in the final few overs. Unbelievably, bearing in mind their earlier plight, Nottinghamshire reached 212 from 60 overs of which Taylor made 63, by far and away his highest score ever, and Johnson 57.

The rest of the day was even worse. Our morale had been severely dented, and we made a bad start in our run chase. Then Greig and Graves took us to 159 for three, and for a while we regained the expectation of success we had had earlier in the day. But we lost three wickets to consecutive balls and finished up four runs short of Nottinghamshire's score. Victory had been hovering within our grasp, and that made defeat – with its rich stigma of failure – even harder to bear. We had reached rock bottom.

Greig drove his Jaguar very fast back down the motorway while I sat in the back, fearful for my life and contemplating the future with some foreboding.

So spectacular was our mediocrity in 1975 that by the end of August Sussex had scarcely won a match. At one stage we lost eight championship matches in a row, four by an innings inside two days. That we were neither a strong team nor well-balanced was obvious to everyone, especially our opponents, and the absence of Greig and Snow, away on Test duty for much of the summer, further reduced our potency. In short, we were a pushover.

By the time we came to play against Hampshire towards the end of that gloriously hot summer we had accepted our plight and were in surprisingly good spirits for a young team accustomed as we were to defeat. I imagine we must have been quite daunted by the prospect of pitting our wits against the legendary talents of Barry Richards, Gordon Greenidge and Andy Roberts. But, on the other hand, what an honour to play against them with so little to lose. After all, it was surely more satisfying to be plundered by these exotic performers than by, say, David Steele who had been plucked from the obscurity of Northamptonshire and thrust into the England side to blunt the fiery Australian bowling of Lillee and Thomson. What an unlikely hero he turned out to be. Thirty-three years old, grey-haired and bespectacled, an ordinary county professional suddenly elevated to a status he had scarcely dreamed about. Steele of all people was the talk of the town in 1975, almost a cult hero.

At Southampton Hampshire scored 501 for five declared, which was the highest score so far amassed since the 100-over limit on first innings was introduced. Actually Sussex got away with it to some extent because we trapped Richards for a mere 49. However, unfortunately, Greenidge was rather severe on us and launched a major bombardment, choosing to pepper all corners of the field and beyond – including a building site just outside the ground's perimeter wall, into which he struck thirteen sixes, a record for a championship innings. The main concern was whether or not Hampshire's supply of balls would run out.

Naturally we Sussex players hoped that they would and thus relieve us from the onslaught. But every now and then a building worker would lob a ball they had found back over the fence and so play, sadly, was never held up for long. It was a bit like playing cricket in the garden with a next-door neighbour somewhat grumpily picking up balls out of a flower bed and chucking them back over the hedge.

The onslaught continued unabated. In our team that day was a young player called Stephen Hoadley, who had been bowling off-breaks occasionally in the second eleven. Not knowing any better, he begged our captain Peter Graves, "Oh please, please won't you give me a bowl?" For a long time Graves resisted these impassioned overtures, but eventually he relented and gave Hoadley a try. And why not? The rest of us hadn't done much good.

What an over it turned out to be. I have visions now of every other ball disappearing into the building site. *Wisden* says there were 22 runs hit off it.

"Oh please, please take me off," begged Hoadley again at the end of what turned out to be his only over in first-class cricket. But, all the same, what a privilege to bowl it at Greenidge who reached his 50, 100, 150 and 200 with sixes and 250 with a four.

By the end I had spotted a weakness, and one of my well-flighted deliveries deceived him and he was caught on the deep mid-wicket boundary for 259. I felt very proud.

Mercifully the wonderful 100-over rule came to our rescue. Had it been a four-day game, as it would be now, I should think Hampshire would have made 1000. Thank goodness, though, we could all troop off with our heads held high, undaunted by the onslaught. At least it was now our turn to bat. And what fun, I thought, as I strapped on my pads. Andy Roberts. Real pace. What a challenge!

The talk in the dressing room was that, whatever else, we did not want to bowl again in the match. We were certainly not going to try to avoid the follow-on. For this 351 was needed. No, we would bat as stoically as possible in the first innings and then have another go in the second. On no account was any attempt to be made to avoid the follow-on. We obeyed our instructions to the letter.

I walked out to bat in the evening sunlight with my partner Jerry Groome. "Good luck," we said to each other and I made my way as usual to the striker's end. I took guard and watched Roberts mark out his long run-up. Every fielder except Turner at cover point was somewhere behind the wicket, eagerly hoping that I would edge a catch their way. This was the moment I had really been waiting for, my reason for playing. In my mind I was the man who could stave off the scary pace and threat of Roberts.

I settled into my stance as Roberts began to run in, legs beginning to pump, eyes cold. I stood still, every nerve and sinew alert and at the ready as I awaited the arrival of that first deadly missile. Then, all of a sudden, the bowler's rhythm broke up. Roberts, with a look of anguish on his face, pulled up, clutching at his leg. Shouting at his captain, Richard Gilliat, fielding in the slips, he said, "No, I cannot bowl," and began to limp sadly from the field. It was the first time I had ever heard him speak.

My partner, Groome, walked down the pitch towards me with a broad grin on his face. "Well, that's a bit of luck," he said as he watched Roberts slope off to the pavilion and Gilliat try to make up his mind what to do next. For my part I was devastated, deprived as it were of my reason for being there, the whole purpose of opening the batting. "It's taken all the fun out of it," I replied. And then, to make matters even worse, Gilliat threw the ball to Trevor Jesty who bowled teasing little swingers at a gentle medium pace. The contrast could not have been more stark. I never fully recovered from the disappointment and succumbed not long afterwards, caught in the gully.

As a team, though, we did extremely well. According to plan our first innings closed after the allotted 100 overs when we were on 259 for eight, still 242 runs behind. Perfect. We would have to bat again, this time for a day and a bit to save the match.

Our second innings saw one of Sussex's greatest rear-guard actions against all the odds. Yet another collapse, we had had so many all season, was surely on the cards. But no – with gritty resolution we battled it out against medium pace and spin. Sadly, for me, there was no chance of Roberts recovering from his strained leg. It had been a long season for him.

Our second innings score of 524 was not only notable for its size but also for the outstanding strokeplay of Mark Faber who, in scoring 176, displayed his extraordinary talent and sense of timing. He tore into a tiring Hampshire attack, and several players followed his example. Indeed towards the end John Spencer was well on course for the fastest hundred of the season and bombarded the building site almost as much as Greenidge had done on the first day. Admittedly a bowling attack of Gilliat and wicket-keeper Stephenson helped him on his way, but it was still stirring stuff with which to conclude the match and celebrate a draw. There was champagne for us in the dressing room at the end.

Just occasionally mediocrity has its day and is rewarded for its tenacity.

9

THE ODD JOB MAN

In the autumn of 1975 I received an invitation from M.C.C. to make a tour of West Africa for a month after Christmas. I accepted immediately, even though I knew that, as a result, my days as an aspiring insurance broker would be numbered.

"You must go on your tour," my boss said to me, "but I don't think there's any need for you to return to us when it is over. Not enough time for you to get into your stride again." I took the point. My far from illustrious career in Life and Pensions was over. An end to endowments, whole life, reversionary and terminal bonuses and all the trappings of finance and its jargon. I could hardly conceal my delight.

That same evening, with the prospect of unemployment looming over my head prior to the start of the 1976 season, I caught the underground as usual at Tower Hill and stood with my face jammed into the shoulder of a fellow traveller while the train rattled and shook its way through to Gloucester Road where, able to breathe once again, I alighted. I was returning to the room I rented in a small flat off Queens Gate Gardens which I shared with three nurses who were training at the Middlesex Hospital. Despite endless talk of bedpans and bodies it was an arrangement which suited me well. My stay there was untroubled.

That evening, as I walked as usual up Gloucester Road from the underground station, amidst the bustle of shoppers already caught up in the Christmas rush, I stopped outside a flower shop, Pugh and Carr, attracted no doubt by the colourful displays in the window, and noticed there a small advertisement which said simply, 'Odd job man required, apply within.' I was not an impulsive person normally and preferred to have a good look at the bowling before playing any shots, but on this occasion I walked straight into the shop. Ten minutes later I walked out again onto Gloucester Road, looking forward to taking up my position as odd job man and van driver at the end of January. It had helped that Tom Pugh, the managing director of the flower business, had himself played for and captained Gloucestershire in the early sixties and was keen to lend a hand to a fellow cricketer in the winter months. At least I now had something to do when I returned from Africa.

The M.C.C. tour was great fun and a huge success. We played good cricket in the Gambia, Sierra Leone – where I encountered a fast bowler with the hostile name of Stalin Adolf Fraser – Ghana, and Nigeria where Colin Cowdrey, just starting a new career with Barclays Bank, joined the party. We coached hundreds of African children and generally spread the rich spirit of cricket around the continent. It was a wonderful experience for a young player just embarking upon the world of professional cricket. I think this tour with its rich variety of players – Bob Barber, Roger Knight, David Nicholls, Michael Hooper – gave me the leg up I needed and certainly raised my confidence and morale.

So it was with optimism that I crossed the threshold of Pugh and Carr in late January and reported to my new boss, the manageress Mary-Lou. She was slender, pretty with dark hair and rather unusual eyes of different colours. From her I took my orders. Disappointingly the task to which I was assigned was painting the loo in the basement.

But there were good moments, too, during which the two worlds of flowers and cricket gradually became linked together. From time to time, as the daffodils and spring flowers emerged,

Mary-Lou and I walked up to Kensington Gardens with a picnic lunch and sat by the Round Pond, watching the ducks. A visit to the ballet at Covent Garden was, I think, the tell-tale sign of enthusiasm. For all that, true love is a slow process, like second-class mail, filled with uncertainty and without the confidence that the end-product will ever materialise. It was three years before Mary-Lou became my permanent boss and manageress when we got married in London just two weeks after we had beaten Somerset in the final of the Gillette Cup.

Life in the flower world was refreshingly different from the insurance business. For a start I was really busy. It was my task to take the van to Covent Garden market in Nine Elms and load it up with flowers. Gone was the romance of Old Covent Garden and Eliza Dolittle, but the new market was a good training ground for me. Nine Elms was like a giant indoor sports arena smothered in flowers and pot plants. I used to run round it, collecting boxes of daffodils, tulips, roses and bunches of foliage before loading them carefully into the van and returning them to headquarters in Gloucester Road. The haul of flowers would then be dumped onto the pavement in front of the shop, ready to be sorted out by the florists.

The rusty – only just roadworthy – blue van became a part of my life for two months. I drove it round London, fetching and carrying during the day, and took it home at night. If I was going out anywhere I usually travelled in the van despite the fact that its exterior was rusting away and the passenger door only opened from the outside. And the van did achieve notoriety one night in late February.

I had been out to dinner and, driving the van as usual, we went on afterwards to a West End night club. In truth I wasn't a great clubbing sort of person, never feeling entirely at home on the dance floor or with a drink in my hand, but on this occasion I did my best to enter into the swing of things, not least because my van was a popular attraction in which, surprisingly, several of the party wanted a ride. They were gluttons for punishment. Anyway after a couple of hours, a few drinks and a little dancing, it was clearly time to go home. Most of my original passengers had already left, perhaps sensing that one journey in the van was enough. "Anyone want a lift home?" I shouted to make myself heard above the din. In the background I heard an American female voice pipe up, "Yes please." "Great," I said, "so long as you don't mind riding in an old van."

So together we climbed the stairs out of the basement and emerged into the night and on to the street at the top. It was about two o'clock in the morning. As we walked down the road, to my surprise, photographers suddenly pounced on us. They appeared, as if by magic, from doorways and side alleys and started clicking frantically. "Good heavens, what's going on?" I said, dazzled by the camera flashes. It was then that I turned to my friend and asked her who she was. "Caroline Kennedy," she said softly. I gulped. I had volunteered to give the late President's daughter a lift home in the van, not a responsibility I was expecting when the evening began.

We made a rush to take refuge in the vehicle, cameras still clicking, and – despite the passenger door not opening properly – we clambered in. By some miracle I managed to get the van started and we set off, photographers in hot pursuit. I pulled out into Jermyn Street and right into St James's Street, at the top of which the lights were mercifully green. Down Piccadilly at speed to Hyde Park corner, first exit down Constitution Hill with Buckingham Palace on our right. It seemed we had shaken off our pursuers, or they had lost interest. But then, as we were navigating the roundabout in front of the Palace, the passenger door, which from the inside had for some time been permanently jammed, suddenly flew open. By some miracle Caroline did not fall out but showed lightning quick reactions in shoving out a hand, grabbing the door handle and pulling it shut. Shortly afterwards, with a sigh of relief, I dropped her safely at her house and kissed her goodnight. I never saw her again. What a shame it is that famous people, without meaning to, cause so much trouble.

Photographs of the van with us both inside appeared on the front page of the *Sunday Mirror* the following weekend and delighted Tom Pugh. "Excellent advertising for the business," he said. In his eyes I had clearly made a success of my winter job.

Caroline and the Flower Pot man

Perhaps this was all good preparation for the new cricket season which began for Sussex at The Oval in a Benson and Hedges zonal match against Surrey. After showing some promising pre-season form I was delighted to be selected to open the batting in our first competitive match. Not only that but Tony Greig allowed me to drive his new car from Hove to London on the understanding that I would drop his overnight bag off at the Waldorf Hotel near Kingsway. It was a white Jaguar. Brand new. There could hardly have been a greater contrast between this prestigious vehicle, albeit sponsored, and the Pugh and Carr van. Greig had an appointment outside London and so entrusted me with its care for the evening.

I took full advantage of this opportunity to show off and made my way swiftly to Egerton Gardens in Knightsbridge where Mary-Lou was celebrating her 21st birthday with a party to which I had been invited. As a special treat, mid-way through the occasion, I took her for a spin around the block. I didn't, of course, pretend that the car was mine but all the same I got the feeling she was impressed. For the first time I began to realise what a bonus it was to have the captain of England in our team.

With the next day's cricket weighing heavily on my mind, I did not stay long at the party and slid quietly away to stay with friends nearby. I avoided hotels if I possibly could.

I arrived at The Oval early on the following day. There I was greeted by Greig whose glowering countenance made it quite clear to me that he was most displeased – very angry, in fact. "Where is my overnight bag?" he bellowed. He was furious. Without pausing to explain my absent-mindedness, I rushed down the stairs and extracted the precious bag from the boot of his car. For a while it seemed that no amount of apologies was going to clear the air so I suffered silently in the corner of the dressing room while Greig used the basin to do his shaving. How could I have forgotten the bag amidst the excitement of the evening? I feared that from now on the white Jaguar was way beyond my reach; I certainly wouldn't be volunteering to drive it again.

Fortunately for me Greig's understandable anger did not last for long, and he wasn't a man to harbour grudges. What I didn't realise at the time was that Greig, from his teenage years, suffered from epilepsy. He had been treated for this very successfully but was dependent upon drugs to keep the condition at bay. It was essential for him to take his tablets every day without fail. My thoughtlessness with the Jaguar had forced him to miss his dose. As I was dependent myself on anti-depressant pills, it does seem ironic, looking back, that it should have been me who was guilty of this thoughtlessness.

It had been a very bad start to my day's cricket and not a great one for Greig, either. The only real hope for me was to start performing better on the field.

Strangely enough, that is what happened. Despite our losing the match quite easily I did make 93 not out and took two wickets, a feat which earned me the man of the match award. In fact I hadn't scored my runs fast enough and Greig, when he joined me at the crease, still looked cross and was immediately bowled trying to force the pace. For all that, I had at long last made my mark on a match and against a good side too.

Our first championship match quickly followed at Ilkeston Cricket Club where, before the end of April, we played Derbyshire. The spectators were few, the weather cold, the pitch slow and the dressing room small. No hot water at the end of the first day made the players grumpy. "Come on then, back to the hotel for a bath." It was here on the second day, having survived the impressive new-ball attack of Hendrick and Ward that I encountered the slow left-arm spin bowling of Freddie Swarbrook. The previous year at Hove on a wet pitch he had emulated Underwood by taking nine for 20 in ten overs, bowling Derbyshire to victory and winning the award for the best bowling figures of the summer. Now at Ilkeston he was trying to pick up from where he had left off so I was taking no chances.

He began his spell with a ball which must have slipped out of his hand. It bounced three or four times before reaching Eddie Barlow at slip. "Bad luck, Fred," someone shouted as the umpire signalled a wide. Swarbrook wiped his hand on the ground and flannels to rid himself of any unwanted moisture and prepared to bowl again. This time the ball shot out of his hand and flew just over my head and wicket-keeper Bob Taylor's too. Apologetically we took two runs. The over continued in much the same vein, and I became increasingly uncomfortable because, although I was the beneficiary, I didn't like to see a fellow professional being tortured by self-doubt and mocked by a small number of spectators.

This was my first experience of the cricketing 'yips', the unexplained and sudden inability to control the ball. One moment Swarbrook was healthy and happy and taking all those wickets at Hove; then, in a trice, he had lost it. His livelihood was going up in smoke.

Swarbrook battled with his demons. He practised in the nets where he could bowl perfectly. Yet, when confronted by a real batsman in a match, the demons returned, the palms and fingers sweaty and control lost. The disease struck others, but never so viciously as it did Swarbrook.

Geoff Miller, who was also playing in the match at Ilkeston, tells an endearing story of Fred visiting a hypnotist who suggested he put a pebble in his pocket and rub it with his left hand prior to bowling. Full of hope, Fred pursued these tactics but sadly to no avail.

Sportsmen of all sorts live on a knife-edge, balanced precariously between success and failure. Nobody will notice a performer who slides into obscurity when natural ability abandons them and leaves them with nothing to fall back on. I don't think Swarbrook ever really recovered.

A few years later we met up again in Kimberley, South Africa where he was looking after the grounds, coaching and playing club cricket as a batsman. I'm sure he never bowled again or even wanted to. That dream was over. He had moved on to a new world without pebbles where his left-arm spin had faded away to a distant memory. Only the triumphs would be recalled. Professional cricket can be a fickle beast.

I suppose, as with the episode of Tony Greig's pills, there was an irony about this unhappy incident at Ilkeston – for, while Fred was wrestling unsuccessfully with the mental agony of bowling, I had now been taking Lithium for several years to stabilise my fluctuating moods. Successful, too, had been this inexpensive, therapeutic drug and, although my cricket had not yet been notably productive, at least I was still playing and giving myself a chance. Regular blood tests suggested that the pills, which I took morning and evening, like brushing my teeth, were doing the trick.

The beginning of the 1976 season signalled my first real run of good form since I had set foot upon the professional stage as long ago as 1970. From Ilkeston, where we won the match comfortably and I scored a few useful runs on a tricky pitch against Alan Ward and Mike Hendrick, we travelled back south to the relative warmth of Hove and our second championship match, against Surrey.

Against the formidable attack of Arnold, Jackman, Pocock and Intikhab, I batted for hours with defence and safety uppermost in my mind. Whatever anyone might say, batting is very much harder than bowling and for me an activity of great intensity. The threat of execution comes with every ball and, when it happens, the shock of dismissal and departure is hard to bear. I felt sick when I got out and found it difficult to endure the stigma of such public failure. Back in the safety of the dressing-room and among the belongings of one's cricket case, there would follow a period of mourning as if there had been a death in the family. Eventually recovery, usually in the form of a cup of tea gripped with a shaking hand, came to the rescue.

On this occasion against Surrey I batted it out without flourish or flamboyance for 98 overs, at the end of which I stood firm on the threshold of my maiden century. I was tantalisingly poised with 98 runs to my name. The fielders were still clustered all around me as if I had just come in. The England off-spinner, Pocock, was the bowler. A series of prods greeted the first few balls of his new over. I was in an hypnotic trance which excluded all attacking shots.

And then it happened. A well-flighted ball brought me forward, prodding again. But this time the combination of extra bounce and a smidgen of spin deceived me, and I edged the ball into Roope's very safe hands at short leg. It was all over, an epic performance though one which did little to stir up the brave spectators in the deck chairs. The Surrey celebration was muted. I think some of them were sad to see me go, especially the bowlers whose rhythm had remained undisturbed for so long. The applause from the pavilion was polite and sympathetic – it always was – before my recovery period began. An unrestful night without sleep followed. It was impossible to switch off after such a lengthy spell of concentration.

The following year I did cross the barrier and scored my first century. It was against Warwickshire at Hove. A week later I scored another, against Gloucestershire at Cheltenham, the first time Mary-Lou came to watch me at an away match. At last I was on my way, though I suspected I had hardly solved the mystery.

But at least by the end of 1976 I was making a contribution. Throughout June, July and August it was like playing abroad, so hot was the sunshine and firm the pitches. I scored exactly 1000 runs that year and was awarded my county cap. On the cricket field at least I was finally becoming more than an odd job man.

Sussex rose to the heights of tenth position in the county championship and came within a whisker of winning the John Player Sunday League, only failing at the last hurdle when Warwickshire proved too much for us. For the first time in my career I was not playing for a team that expected to lose every match. It seemed that Sussex had turned the corner – and so had I.

10

ONE BAD DAY, TWO GOOD

Throughout 1977 and on into 1978 the good days were gradually beginning to outnumber the bad ones. This is the story of one bad day, horrible even, followed by two good days, all in the same summer of 1978.

The first was in May, on one of those damp and overcast days when the sea fret hangs hauntingly over the County Ground at Hove. In these unpromising conditions Sussex were playing Middlesex in a Benson and Hedges zonal qualifying match which would decide which teams would progress to the quarter finals. I stood at the sea end, nervously tapping my bat on the ground as I prepared to face the first ball of the day from Wayne Daniel, Middlesex's huge West Indian fast bowler. With pulses of mist and drizzle rolling in off the sea Daniel, as he paced out his long run-up, would disappear and reappear again disconcertingly as the fog swirled about him.

"Play," shouted the umpire at last. I heard the heavy tread of Daniel's feet as he roared in down the hill and emerged from the gloom like a train from a tunnel. He bore down on me menacingly, over came his arm as he propelled the ball with fearsome power into the unforgiving pitch in front of him. I heard something hit the ground but, seeing nothing in the gloom, could do no more than thrust my arm up in front of my face in self-defence. The ball crashed into my wrist, sending a numbing sensation fizzing up my arm. It was a withering moment. I dropped my bat and shouted, not at anyone in particular and certainly not at Daniel with whom I was determined to remain friends if at all possible. The nearest fielder to me was Clive Radley at short-leg, a man well used to suffering at the hands of fast bowlers and who wore a battle-hardened expression on his face. He knew what it was like to be in the trenches. "Horrible game at times," he said, "and that's only the first ball." This remark was not helpful.

Before long a circle of players surrounded me, wondering whether I would do the sensible thing and retire hurt. Spray and ice were brought out from the pavilion, all of which served to waste time. "Never show them you're hurt," I was told as a youngster. In this instance I couldn't see the point of pretence, and anyway I was quite enjoying the sympathy. Eventually, some fifteen minutes later, with the sea fret thinning out a bit, the match continued and I faced Daniel's second ball which, more by luck than judgement, collided with my bat and was deflected to long leg. I ran a very slow single.

At the other end I was greeted by an old friend, John Langridge, a first-class umpire of many years and in his day as an opening batsman for Sussex the scorer of more than 30,000 runs. John was an ally, somebody who understood and could be relied upon. "How would you play Daniel?" I asked him while the big man was walking back to his mark. "I'd stay up this end," he answered with a smile. I took his advice.

It wasn't long before Daniel struck. This time he dug one in short at my opening partner, Mendis, who cut the ball imperiously off the middle of the bat, only to see it plucked from the air athletically and quite brilliantly by Featherstone in the gully. It brought Stewart Storey in to bat. After a distinguished career as an all-rounder with Surrey, Storey had joined Sussex to lend experience to a youngish side. This was his first match at Hove. As non-striker I watched with interest as Daniel pounded in again and unleashed a brute of a ball which reared up in front of Storey, striking him a fierce blow on the hand and ricocheting onto his shoulder from whence it struck him on the side of the head. As if that was not bad enough the ball then ballooned up into the air in the direction of cover who, running back a few yards, caught it comfortably. Storey, dazed and injured, had to return to the pavilion where a hard-hearted member suggested that he return to Surrey. In fact he went to hospital for emergency repairs to his painful wounds.

Peter Graves, who replaced Storey, somehow managed to elude Daniel for a bit and was patiently trying to make some progress against Mike Selvey at the other end when a good-length ball reared up at him viciously and he took a nasty blow on the fingers. Like me he dropped his bat in disapproval and ripped off his glove. It was quite clear from the look of his finger that no amount of bravery would repair the damage and Graves, with a forlorn look of resignation, retired also to the pavilion and onwards to hospital where he joined Storey.

The damage to the Sussex innings – and to morale – was now irreversible. It was simply a battle for survival and a matter of coming out of this grisly ordeal alive. Sussex had never done very well in the Benson and Hedges competition, and nothing that day was going to reverse our dismal track record. Shell-shocked and shattered, we mustered 60 runs in all from 26 turbulent overs of which Daniel bowled just nine and took six for 17 in as explosive a spell as could ever be imagined. Tearing down the hill as he did, he simply laid waste all who stood before him, including me, the innings' top-scorer with 17. I lost my leg stump in the end and could be thankful that no more permanent damage was done.

As it turned out, the outcome of the game was not a total disaster. Such was the mathematical complexity of the competition's regulations that, for Sussex to qualify with Middlesex for the quarter finals, it was important that Middlesex achieved their target in as few overs as possible and preferably losing some wickets along the way. They scored the runs in just eight overs for the loss of two wickets and so, despite the battleground and casualties, Sussex progressed with Middlesex to the next stage of the competition. Sadly we got no further, a familiar story.

We did somewhat better in the Gillette Cup, reaching the final at Lord's where we had to play our fierce rivals Somerset who, with Viv Richards, Ian Botham and Joel Garner, were hot favourites to win. On our way to the final we had out-manoeuvred Suffolk and Staffordshire, the latter by just two runs, and got the better of Yorkshire at Headingley in a watery ten-over bash. Only in the semi-final against Lancashire had we really come into our own and played with complete confidence. We had got to the final without much form to go on.

On the morning of the match my normal routine was disrupted as, from the early hours, I failed to sleep. Exasperated by this uncalled-for restlessness, and with the airing cupboard now but a distant memory, I got up, dressed and drove off into London from our hotel near Regents Park. I had no particular destination in mind but allowed myself to be led. Not unexpectedly the streets of London were clear of traffic at that time of day, and I made quick progress towards the City. There I stopped near St Paul's Cathedral and parked the car.

The sun was coming up amidst the spires and skyscrapers. A single bell was ringing; I was just in time for the early service at 7.30 a.m. Despite its being a bright Saturday morning in September the cathedral was almost deserted, and it took me some time to find the small side chapel where prayers would be said. In fact I was not the only one there; two old ladies, clearly regulars, were already seated in their pews. At the back was an old man of dishevelled and unkempt appearance. I took him to be a tramp and, although sympathetic to his plight, it was the smell surrounding him and his ragged clothing that steered me to a seat some distance away.

The priest arrived, and the service began. I am ashamed to say that I prayed fervently for Sussex and gave God quite a detailed run through of the day's play as I saw it. Why I should have expected God to support Sussex any more than Somerset, I can't imagine but for half an hour He was bombarded with Sussex propaganda.

After the service the old tramp spoke to me briefly as I left the chapel. In a surprisingly educated voice he wished me well for the day and asked me how I was going to fill it. Holding my breath as I hurried out, I told him. "Have fun," he said, and that was that.

By the time I reached Lord's there was already a buzz about the ground. Having forfeited my breakfast in favour of God, I felt in need of sustenance before tackling the enemy and was much fortified by a sandwich which I grabbed not far from the Grace Gates. I ate it in the dressing room as the rest of the team began to arrive. There still seemed to be a long time to go before the match was due to start. It was like arriving unnecessarily early for a dentist's appointment with too much time to consider the pain which the treatment might inflict. How much better just to get on with things without the tortuous preamble and all the shilly-shallying about.

The match started in an unusual way. Imran Khan, our star bowler, in his enthusiasm and with heart thumping fast, bowled a wild opening over which consisted of a succession of wides, no balls and deliveries that the batsman hit for four. At the end of it there were 14 runs on the board. I watched all this from square leg and consoled myself, not for the first time, by concluding that often it was a mistake to peak too early. Fortunately we had a long way to go.

It wasn't long before Arnold Long, our captain, decided that slow bowling might be more effective than fast. Therefore, unexpectedly early in the match, he signalled to me that I should loosen up and get ready to bowl. In the event I kept warming up, on standby, for what seemed like an eternity, while my fellow spinner, Giles Cheatle, slow left-arm, got cracking from the nursery end. At last and with the Somerset score nearing 100, I was called into action.

I felt sick as I walked towards the stumps at the pavilion end and, despite some kind and encouraging words from umpire Dickie Bird, I fervently wished I could be removed from Lord's and placed back in my pew at St Paul's, stench notwithstanding, and be safe again. By now both batsmen, Viv Richards and Ian Botham, were beginning to flex their muscles, threatening to attack the bowling vigorously. I bustled in off my short run and bowled to Richards. Given the importance of the match and the state of the game, even he would surely have to take my bowling more seriously than he usually might. Indeed he did, treating me with some respect at least and, oddly enough, so too did Botham. They curbed their natural flair and allowed me to settle. Then an extraordinary thing happened.

With the tension mounting, I began my fifth over, I think it was. The first ball was directed by mistake down the leg-side. Richards swung at it but not with the usual conviction of the master he was, and it caught the top edge of his bat whence it spiralled high into the air in the direction of Geoff Arnold at deep square leg. There was a hideous moment as the ball dropped from the sky. Arnold stood there impassive and, despite the pressures of the world being temporarily thrust upon him, he safely caught the ball. For me, rarely could there have been a more joyous moment as players rushed to congratulate the fielder. Mercifully, nobody considered hugging me; I should have hated that.

Somerset never quite recovered from this wretched blow and lost their momentum and way. After 60 overs they had to be content with the relatively modest score of 207 for seven. I took one more wicket, that of Vic Marks for 4, and finished with two for 21 from 12 overs, a miserly performance and one with which the tramp would surely have been well pleased for me.

Now it was time for batting and the run chase. I opened the innings with Gehan Mendis, and together we had to contend with the fast bowling of Garner and Botham. Normally I would have been outclassed and outscored by Mendis, whose hooking and cutting had few rivals. But that day, for some reason, I held my own and, when I was got out for 44, my share of our opening partnership of 93 was greater than that of Mendis. Maddeningly I was lured to my demise by the energetic Botham. He banged yet another ball onto the Lord's turf and induced me to hook. The ball struck the bat high up on the blade and spooned up pathetically to mid-on where Peter Roebuck took a simple catch. It was the end for me, and now all I could do was watch and cheer the team on.

There are few things worse than sitting in a pavilion during a run chase. The balance between trying to uplift and console is exhausting, so on this occasion I gave up and went to have a bath, putting my trust in the batsman to see us home.

The baths at Lord's are both individual and large – a communal plunge bath was never part of the scheme of things at this great ground. For nearly ten minutes I relaxed in the warm water and began to calm down, oblivious to all that was going on outside. I couldn't even hear the crowd.

After a suitable interval and, draping a large white towel around my dripping body, I returned to the dressing room. I was immediately struck by the mournful silence that accompanies disaster. Imran Khan and Javed Miandad, our two magical players from Lahore and Karachi, were sitting disconsolately together in the corner, staring into space. Both still had their pads strapped on but clearly neither was waiting to bat. They had done their best and failed. The score had slumped to 110 for four.

From this low point and with the sun already beginning to cast long shadows over the ground, Paul Parker and Paul Phillipson, both men of Sussex though born elsewhere, began to repair the damage. They were helped in their task by Botham who, in his great enthusiasm and remember he was only a youngster then, got overexcited by the occasion and bowled erratically – a succession of long-hops and half-volleys which got us going. The grateful batsmen both took full advantage of this good fortune and began to pull things round.

So well did the two of them play that victory did not take long in coming, and Sussex at last lifted up the Gillette Cup once more, celebrating its superiority in the one-day game. There was much rejoicing. 'More easily now,' John Woodcock wrote in *The Times*, 'Sussex can face the future rather than lament the past.'

For me, to have scored 44 runs and taken two wickets including that of Viv Richards, as well as being part of a winning team, it was indeed a triumph. But there were many responsible for the triumph, not least, I think, the tramp at St Paul's whose calming influence had given a sense of perspective to a big day. For all my anxiety, I had had fun.

A second triumph came just six weeks later in South Africa. Despite having a good day at Lord's, 1978 had not been a fluent season for me. I had stumbled from match to match tormented by my own batting technique which encouraged the opposition bowlers more than it did me. I decided that I needed to sharpen up my game by playing cricket professionally for a season in the Orange Free State, South Africa.

I went out with my wife Mary-Lou, whom I had married just two weeks after the Gillette Cup triumph. We lived in Bloemfontein, and there I played for and captained the railway club, Schoeman Park. I was warmly welcomed into the world of Afrikaans-speaking people whose culture was sheltered from the outside world through the cover of the government's apartheid policies. Unashamedly at the time, I used this abhorrent system to improve my cricket, such was my obsession with the game. Africans were strictly forbidden to use the facilities of the cricket club which stood idle for much of the day, and woe betide any suggestion that they should use our nets. This was strictly Whites Only. It would seem that the Dutch Reformed Church was similarly indoctrinated and unwilling to share its God with the natives. Despite all this we made a great friend in an African called Solomon who, as caretaker of the small block of flats where we lived, gave us a rousing welcome each day and would always help Mary-Lou with the shopping.

One of the clever features of apartheid was its cunning camouflage behind which South Africa could conceal its inhuman side from its visitors. That, I presume, is why it went unchecked for so long. Not that I cared much at the time because I had been selected to play for the Orange Free State against Western Province at the Ramblers Club in Bloemfontein. This was what really mattered to me.

It was the first round of the Datsun Shield, the equivalent of our Gillette Cup at home. Free State cricket was not considered to be strong and was certainly very much inferior to the might of Western Province. It was not expected to be a close contest. All the same it was a challenge, and fun for us in Bloemfontein to pit our wits against the strength of cricket in the Western Cape.

Under our team manager and coach, Ewie Cronje, we prepared ourselves with much care for the match and tried to unravel the mysteries of field placing and running between the wickets. Fielding practice was intense, though not quite employing the complex drills that are now routine; by the time the big day arrived, we certainly did not expect to drop a catch. Ewie's two boys, Franz and Hansie, aged 11 and 9 respectively, were our keenest and most loyal supporters and joined in with the preparations whenever possible. This visit from Western Province was a big event for Free State cricket and for Bloemfontein, where the only sport really understood by the locals was rugby. Cricket normally came a distant second.

Sunshine and a cloudless sky greeted the teams on the day of the match. The pitch, the closely cropped outfield and weather conditions all looked deeply sympathetic to batsmen. Despite this it came as no surprise when Robbie East, our captain, won the toss and invited his counterpart, Hylton Ackerman, to bat first. The idea was, I suppose, to keep the game going for as long as possible. The Western Province line-up was formidable: Kirsten, Lamb, Swart, Le Roux and Omar Henry. A large score was on the cards as we set about our task beneath the hot African sun.

Yet the Western Province batsmen never quite got into their stride. Class was kept on a tight rein and true pedigree was not given its chance to blossom. By the time I came on to bowl my gentle off-spinners, the batting had already lost its rhythm and so was unsettled. It was made worse for them when I had Allan Lamb caught behind down the leg-side for 7, given out by a local umpire who sported a spectacular moustache – grey, crisp and pointed – and with whom I had struck up an important and productive friendship. Lamb did not think he had hit the ball, which indeed he probably hadn't, but that's batting for you. Justice and injustice are close companions in cricket's restless struggle.

Western Province slid smoothly into disarray after that. Nobody was really able to get going and even Garth Le Roux, who loved to hit the spinners miles, was restrained and let me get away with it. Later at Sussex, where he became one of my closest cricketing friends, he would shudder at the thought of this match and especially at the timid way my bowling was treated. Western Province collapsed and were bowled out for 144 in considerably less than the allotted 60 overs.

Back in the pavilion we strapped on our pads while Cronje paced up and down the dressing room, filling us with much-needed confidence and calming our nerves. We had two Le Rouxs of our own in our side to open the batting, Raymond and Darryl, and they strode out to do battle with the pride of the Orange Free State in their hearts.

I was all ready to bat next and did not have to wait long, thank goodness. A wicket fell early, and I was thrust on to the stage before any wriggling worms of doubt had the chance to take a hold. Nonetheless my legs still shook somewhat, not from fear of injury even though Le Roux was a very hostile and fast bowler – menacing and big – but more from fear of failure, the devil which dogs every professional sportsman.

Why on earth I should have played well that day, I will never know. From the outset the ball plummeted into the middle of my bat. Usually it didn't. In fact, in my career, there were many more days of failure than success. So much so that failure is one of the few things about which I count myself an expert.

I had waited years for this sort of day. I played a cut shot at a wide ball from Le Roux and it almost went for six, an unremarkable event you might think, but it would have been my first proper six in a big match. As it was, I had to wait until Ilford in 1981 when, by mistake, I hit a full toss from Norbert Phillip over David Acfield's head and into the startled Essex spectators in front of the small pavilion. It took them by surprise as it did me.

Later in my Free State innings the fielders even began to drop deeper to give me a single and get me away from the strike. This had never happened before, nor indeed has it since. For just about the only time in my career I felt powerful. My good fortune continued that day and, with the sun beginning to lose its strength and the lager flowing freely in the crowd, the Orange Free State won a glorious victory. I was chaired off the field, not a comfortable experience and not one I would recommend as a means of transport over any distance. I did not have far to go, however, and leading my fan club was a young Hansie Cronje who with his brother Franz raced onto the ground at the end, accompanying me to the safety of the pavilion. I won the man of the match award for 93 runs and three wickets.

When later I returned with Mary-Lou to our flat, we were greeted by Solomon who wanted to hear all about it. He insisted on carrying my cricket case upstairs.

11

FISHING

Arthur Ransome, most famous as the author of children's books, was also a distinguished fishing writer. It was his great passion, giving him more pleasure than his other achievements. His masterpiece, *Rod and Line*, was published in 1929, the year of my mother's birth.

The book starts with a beautifully constructed sentence to which most fishermen will relate with a smile. 'The pleasures of fishing are chiefly to be found in rivers, lakes and tackle-shops and, of the three, the last is the least affected by the weather.' On trips north to fish the rivers of Scotland, rarely do I fail to stop off at John Norris's tackle shop in Penrith where a good hour can be spent stocking up on all manner of kit and equipment, much of it superfluous to the needs of fishing but all of it part of the rich culture none the less.

But it is on the river bank, within sight and sound of running water and the scenery that surrounds it, that I am most at home. We all need to relax and to rest our souls somehow, and this is how I have chosen to do so more or less since the first occasion I caught a fish.

It was in October 1962, towards the end of a sunny autumn day fishing for grayling on the River Coln at Fairford in Gloucestershire. I was eight years old, and my father and brother had moved upstream to try their luck elsewhere. They left me standing by a blackberry bush, armed with a fishing rod and line. I repeatedly chucked the line and fly into the river and bombarded the pool in front of me. The sun was losing its strength, beginning to go down in the west, when I once again retrieved my line for another cast, only to encounter a resistance which I took to be the river bed. One of life's most thrilling moments occurs when the river bed starts to move and squirm.

I pulled with all my strength and a small silver fish flew out of the water and landed in the blackberry bush behind me. It took a while to unravel the line, the fish and rod all wrapped up amidst the prickly obstruction. That was my first fish, a grayling, about the size of a small herring. I patted it with pride all the way back to Oxford, where I was at school, and there sadly had to bid it farewell.

From then onwards I never needed any encouragement to fish. Rivers and water are in my blood. There are few bridges on my travels across the country over which I have not leant and peered down into the water, from small streams to the mighty Trent and Severn in flood. There is something mesmerising about water, its power and independence. The incoming and ebbing tide has the same effect upon me. I've seen large sea trout stranded in flood-water in the River Arun and vast pike lazing in backwaters waiting to breed. And it's not just fish. I've seen an osprey fishing for trout on the River Oykel in Scotland; the flash of a kingfisher flying low over the water in the south and the dipper bobbing about amongst the rocks; otters in Scotland playing on the far bank. Fishing is a peaceful pursuit and unsettles wild creatures less than most. That is its charm; that is why I so enjoy it.

For most of my life, and certainly since I've been able to drive, rod, fishing bag and boots have been more or less permanent companions. Opportunities to fish or spend time by a river have rarely been missed.

To some extent cricket and fishing exist as friendly and favourable companions. Fine weather usually meant playing cricket whereas wet weather filled the rivers with water and the fisherman's heart with hope. On one such occasion, when we visited Bristol, a city renowned for damp conditions, I persuaded Geoff Arnold and Gehan Mendis, Sussex team-mates, to join me on a fishing trip to Castle Combe in Wiltshire, on a tributary of the Avon. It was pouring with rain as we trudged across fields to reach the water's edge. Armed with much wet-weather kit to combat the deluge, my friends watched stoically in silence as I prepared to fish. If I had been determined to introduce beginners to the world of fishing, I could not have chosen a worse day. Already, and it was not yet midday, my companions had half an eye on the hotel nearby, its log fire and bar, and they would have been heading that way but for an improbable moment of success in the river. I hooked and landed a small trout. "Not very big," I shouted to my companions and, as I did so, displayed my fish with pride. "It's early days," I said, "so let's put him back. Plenty more in the river, I'm sure." These words would come back to haunt me as the wet day wore on.

Despite my modest triumph Mendis and Arnold wisely sought out the bar while I continued to fish with enthusiasm. From time to time they would emerge from the hotel's warmth and make unhelpful suggestions, egged on by a drink or two. "Dynamite might help." I didn't laugh. My sense of humour had been washed away down stream.

It wasn't until later in the evening that I had any more success, by which time the cricketers had long since returned to Bristol and the comfort of their hotel there. In the end on a rugged day my perseverance was rewarded by four good trout. The following day at lunchtime, another wet one, I surprised the more-than-willing catering staff with a bonus for their supplies. The trout were served up in the pavilion at

Bristol and provided an unexpected meal for the players of both teams. Mike Procter tucked in hungrily, but I got the feeling that Zaheer Abbas and Sadiq Mohammed viewed my fish with some suspicion.

Fishermen generally confess that most of their time spent by the water is filled with hope rather than actually catching fish. I was brought up by my father as a trout fisherman trying to deceive fish with flies made mainly from feathers and fur tied around a hook. The process required much casting and waving of the line so as to cover the fishy places in the stream. Much would be caught other than fish: weed and debris, trees and bushes and occasionally oneself, particularly on a windy day. Tangles would be frequent and changes of fly often a necessity, particularly when imbedded in vegetation on the far bank. Much time was spent on recovery and reorganisation.

More recently, though, I have been introduced to salmon fishing. The salmon is the most extraordinary species. They breed right up at the top of rivers or burns and, after hatching, spend some two years feeding voraciously in the river before setting off to rich pastures far away in the sea. Some return as grilse (a small salmon) after a year and others a few years later as mighty salmon. They always come back to the same river, indeed the very same pool in which they were born. When in the river they have only sex on the brain; their stomachs close down and their mind is concentrated on breeding. It is on this return to freshwater they can be caught on a fly, taken probably more in anger than anything else.

It took me a long time to catch my first salmon, weeks and months of unfruitful labour. The day of my first success began badly. It was blowing a gale, and I had been fishing down beneath some trees on the River Don in Aberdeenshire. Because of the wind, my casting was in a mess. Roll casts, spey casts, overhead casts and just hacking the line out, I tried them all; the result was an ungainly muddle splashing inaccurately on the water. My efforts were further hindered when, as I stood in the middle of the river, a branch from an overhanging tree swooped down, grabbed my hat and then flicked it unforgivingly out into the middle of the pool. I loved my hat and had possessed it as part of my fishing equipment for many years and now there it was, picked up by a tree and beginning to drown. I wound in the line vigorously and staggered to one side in my chest-waders before setting off downstream in pursuit of my beloved hat. I used the tip of my rod to poke and prod it, trying to persuade it to come ashore. But all to no avail. My progress was severely impaired by my waders which were not ideal for athletic and fluent motion along the bank. Gradually the hat became waterlogged and began to sink. I gave it up for lost and sadly paddled on downstream, hatless, to the next pool where I would try my luck again.

When I made my next cast, I was not in the best of spirits. I felt naked on top without my hat on my head, and I had yet to catch one of these mysterious fish. The sun had come out and I was beginning to fish in a dreamy sort of way, certainly not concentrating, but at least with the line in the water. Out of the blue I felt a little 'dink-dink' and hooked what I took to be a small trout. It wasn't until the fish began to swim about more strongly that I realised this was the real thing. Eventually, with feelings of anxiety and jubilation, I coaxed a sizeable salmon into my trout net whereupon we sat together on the bank to savour one of life's wonderful moments. To be fair, it wasn't a great moment for the salmon.

I do love fishing. It has a therapeutic effect upon my soul; it lifts my spirits. And it sits quite well with cricket: two sports where, for much of the time, all is quiet until the serenity is interrupted by an explosion of activity. Then the tranquillity of the river, or the cricket, returns. The flow is undisturbed once more.

12

NEW RESPONSIBILITIES

By 1979 life was going rather well for me. Bloemfontein, despite being one of South Africa's more desolate and distant outposts and playing host to the heartbeat of Afrikanerdom and apartheid, was doing me good. I played cricket regularly there and coached in various schools where English was rarely the predominant language. I wrote a newspaper column each week in the local *Daily Mail* which, despite its small circulation, gave me something to think about and allowed me to express my views. I embarked upon a vigorous training programme, mainly running and swimming, with Kepler Wessels and Andy Lloyd of Warwickshire. I practised with them at lunchtime when they would bowl gentle spinners to me, teaching me how to play spin – a skill I had not yet mastered.

My life was changing. I suppose I was growing up. Mary-Lou and I were now young marrieds in Bloemfontein and setting out upon our adventures together. Back at home I had bought a house not far from Brighton in a village called Henfield, where we had lived as a young family 17 years earlier. Inside there were four very small rooms and a staircase; there was just enough space for us to move about in if we were careful. Outside I dug a vegetable garden, which occupied my mind after a tough day's cricket and produced a surprising amount of runner beans, French beans, spinach, potatoes and carrots.

There was nothing very exciting about all this. I was twenty-five years old and settled. Not only that, I was made vice-captain. The captain, Arnold Long, and cricket manager, Tony Buss, had forged an important partnership for Sussex cricket. From the muddle earlier in the decade, the team had been shrewdly and cleverly constructed: Gehan Mendis, Paul Parker and the Wells brothers, all with Sussex backgrounds; Kepler Wessels, Javed Miandad, Imran Khan and Garth Le Roux, from overseas; Geoff Arnold and Chris Waller, from Surrey; and Ian Greig, following in his brother's footsteps. Stewart Storey added experience to the mix, and Tim Booth-Jones from Hastings became an unlikely hero for a short while. Tony Pigott emerged as a tearaway fast bowler while John Spencer remained steady and consistent.

The outcome was a team that had the potential to perform far better than it had done at any time since the early sixties. And indeed it did: fourth in the county championship and semi-finalists in the Gillette Cup.

The vice-captaincy did me no harm, either. I did the 'double' of 1000 runs and 50 wickets, a feat which only Mike Procter and Clive Rice also achieved in that summer of 1979. Even my three games as captain showed promise with a draw and two wins.

In the following winter, spent in Grahamstown in South Africa's Eastern Cape, I was able to look back and savour this successful introduction to leadership. This was just as well for, playing in the league for the University of Grahamstown, I had a rotten time with bat and ball. In one particular match I opened the batting against the University of Port Elizabeth in the annual encounter at St George's Park, a match not notable for polite manners or affable discourse. I made no runs in either innings, a pair, which left me with hours in the stand, pondering my future in the game. Cricket often leaves you with too much time on your hands. My morale was not improved when several of the participants suggested that county cricket really couldn't be all it was cracked up to be.

After a season in South Africa that would have broken the spirit of many a gritty competitor, I nonetheless returned to

England for the summer of 1980 full of hope, trusting that it would all be different back at home in the cold. And it was. In the second match I broke my thumb and was sidelined for six weeks, which gave me plenty of time to dwell upon my role as vice-captain. I was both miserable and bored and excluded from the action; I was surprised by how much I missed playing.

Arnold Long had made it quite clear that he would be retiring at the end of the season so, when I rejoined the side at the end of June, I was more conscious than ever that the captaincy was up for grabs. So I was on my best behaviour and trying to display my talents in the most positive light. Fortunately I failed to emulate my South African form and scored, by my standards, quite freely both with bat and ball.

When Long decided to stand down early in August, I led Sussex for the first time that season. The match, against Northamptonshire at Eastbourne, was an unusual one. I won the toss and Sussex, batting first on a hot day and on a brown pitch, scored more runs than I can ever remember – and with a limit of 100 overs, too. Mendis scored 204, Parker 122, Wessels 97, Imran Khan 4 not out, and I made 26, rather dashingly by my standards, at the beginning of the day. With a few extras added, we made in total 482 for three.

In the bar afterwards I was relaxing over a drink with Garth Le Roux, a big South African who, although not actually playing in the match, had come to watch. We were discussing the frenzied run-scoring, and Garth was rejoicing that he himself did not have to bowl on what appeared to be a paradise for batting, when an oldish lady wandered over in our direction and made it clear she wished to engage us in conversation. Looking at me quite sternly, she came straight to the point. "Mr Barclay," she said, "what does it feel like to be the least successful batsman of the day amidst this run feast?" It was neither the most tactful question nor one which was particularly easy to answer. I was stuck for a reply, but during the lull Le Roux came to my rescue. He drew himself up to his full height and, towering above the little lady, said, "Madam, I would have you know that this is my captain you are talking to, our leader, and I think you should also be reminded that even Napoleon himself, in all his glory, did not fire too many shots either." The lady was silenced. My shortcomings were justified and my position as captain vindicated. Not surprisingly, after all that batting, we won the match comfortably. Imran bowled well as he tended to at Eastbourne; in fact everyone did, and by the end I felt I had got a small tick in the approval box.

Most of you who have played some cricket over the years will know that the game has a funny knack of getting its own back, taking revenge. Strange it is how success is so frequently followed by a downturn in fortune. That was certainly the case in my early days of captaincy. Just two weeks elapsed between the Northampton match and a promising week's cricket at Hove against Surrey and Middlesex, local rivals of course.

For some reason, inexplicable so far as I can see, on winning the toss in both matches I elected to field first, and this in fine weather and on good pitches. Very strange. It is just possible that there may have been some deep inner psychological reason for the decisions. I was the Sussex opening batsman, and Sylvester Clarke of Surrey and Wayne Daniel of Middlesex were very fast and intimidating opening bowlers. Maybe I was taking the opportunity to put off something horrid till tomorrow.

Mike Brearley, the Middlesex captain and opening batsman, was also aware of this element of the captain's predicament.

In the event both decisions backfired badly and put Sussex firmly on the back foot. Good preparation and the wise assessment of evidence contribute to sound decision-making and good leadership. But as Brearley reminded me, over a drink in the evening, the outcome of decisions is largely out of our control once they have been taken. Despite his broad intellect Brearley's approach to the game was nonetheless a simple one and easily understood by his players. That was his greatest strength as a captain.

To a small extent I got away with these mistakes. Although Surrey did indeed take advantage of my generosity and beat us easily, Middlesex, expecting to clinch the county championship at Hove, had not reckoned with a very stubborn Sussex rearguard action led by Wessels and supported by Colin Wells and Le Roux. In fact we all made some runs, and the match was drawn. Middlesex had to wait for one more game before claiming the title.

From a position of strength my reputation as captain had by now slid ominously downhill. Questions were being asked about my tactical know-how. The committee couldn't work it out and neither could anyone else.

I remembered what John Snow had said about captaincy at Old Trafford back in 1974. Tony Buss, leading Sussex in the absence of Greig, lost the toss and subjected Snow and the rest of us to a day in the field. In fact Snow took an early wicket, Barry Wood it was, and, as Frank Hayes walked out to bat, our fast bowler, wanting to rub in his displeasure with Buss, shouted out, "Come on, chaps, let's see if we can trap another." Lancashire finished on 304 for four.

Back in the dressing room Snow spoke his mind. "All captains should be banned," he said.

The upshot of my inconsistent and erratic foray into the world of leadership was that, shortly after the last match of the 1980 season, I was summoned to the chairman of Sussex's flat in Hove and offered the captaincy for the following summer.

Within a few days Mary-Lou and I boarded a plane bound for Sydney – she pregnant and I with John Snow's words still ringing in my ears.

13

UNDER THE EYE OF THE SELECTORS

In Sydney I was the epitome of the county cricketer abroad, trying to fill in the time usefully between cricket seasons. We lived in the eastern suburbs, in Coogee to be more accurate, within walking distance of the sea in which we swam regularly. We did our shopping mainly in Grace Brothers and Coles New World and made friends with people in Paddington who had a successful look in their eye. On Saturdays I played for and captained Waverley in the league and during the week coached at Scots College, Cranbrook and Sydney Grammar School where I taught them cricket and they taught me Australian. I like to think we learnt a lot.

After a hesitant start the cricket went well, and I felt quite at home with my new team. It all suited me nicely. We played in various suburbs: Penrith, Petersham, Bankstown and, a little smarter, Mosman and Manley. The cricket introduced me to parts of Sydney I might otherwise have avoided. And on January 9th at St Mary's hospital, Paddington, Georgina Barclay was born. There's no doubt that luck plays a large part in life, and Georgie got off to a bad start. A nasty cough after ten days turned out to be whooping cough so she was packed off to the Princess Alexandra Hospital for Children in Parramatta where she spent the next seven weeks. There was no cure for whooping cough in one so small, only the love and care of the nursing staff and access to oxygen when needed. Mary-Lou wasn't too well either at this stage so I used to trek across Sydney every evening to feed Georgina. I eventually mastered the bottle, only small amounts, from which the tiny baby began to gather strength. With her lungs and brain miraculously intact we were all set to travel home by March 1981, ready to settle down in good time for the new season.

While in Australia I spent a fair amount of time in thought, mulling over the campaign ahead. I knew we had the players from which to build upon the performances of 1979 and 1980; there was no doubting our potential. The training and practice sessions had to become more intense and discussion periods, with all the squad together, more regular and effective. I was determined to build up a spirit that would hold together under pressure. I felt full of energy and ready to take on anyone.

In early April I visited the club's GP in Hove for my routine medical examination prior to the season. I was feeling so well and excited about the forthcoming summer that I calmly produced from my pocket, as if it were a normal thing to do, the lithium tablets which I had been taking for ten years. "I'm sure I can do without these," I said, placing them on his desk. "I feel fine now." And that was that. No questions asked. And the pills disappeared out of my life. I left them there and thought nothing of it. Within a few days the season was under way and the fixtures queuing up.

And my goodness we did play well and with an intensity of purpose not seen in Sussex for years. Matches were won in all competitions; indeed it wasn't until towards the end of June that we first lost one, in the Sunday league against Northamptonshire. There was a buzz about the team and an indefinable electricity that lifted performances. Sussex had got it. Even Bill Alley, the Test match umpire, noticed it. "I reckon you're all on pills," he said to me one day when I was preparing to bowl. I didn't like to tell him that this was just about the only time in my career when I was off the pills.

But the schedule of county cricket could be punishing at times; as captain of Sussex, I was playing cricket for 27 of the 30 days in June 1981. Then, when the county finally had a three-day break in the first week of July, three of us – Gehan Mendis, Paul Parker and I – were selected to play for a Test and County Cricket Board eleven against the touring Sri Lankans at Trent Bridge.

It was an important game for us – it was our first glimpse of recognition by the England selectors, who were all due to be present at the match – and also for Sri Lanka, who were hoping and expecting to be granted full Test match status in the near future.

I had been asked to captain the team and was rather

nervous at the prospect. It was one thing to captain a group of people you knew well – the Sussex team were just about getting used to me by now – but quite another to lead a bunch of relative strangers in a 'one-off' match. What on earth would they make of me? Gatting, Emburey, Downton and a young Simon Hughes from Durham University were the Middlesex contingent; Paul Allott and Paul Newman were young fast bowlers from Lancashire and Derbyshire, and Wayne Larkins and Jim Love batsmen from Northamptonshire and Yorkshire. There was lots of talent there both from within the England team and on the fringe.

As I travelled up with Parker and Mendis, I gave the match a lot of thought on the journey, bouncing ideas off them as we went. It was late when we left our favourite bistro off the Old Brompton Road in London so it was unlikely that I would bump into any of my new team-mates in Nottingham until the next day. I still wasn't quite clear how I would handle things and went to bed unsettled and hoping for overnight inspiration.

It is a curious thing about captains that they mostly wish to make their mark and stamp their personality on proceedings at an early stage. But some try too hard, and I came into that category at Nottingham. With Sussex I always said a few words before each session, and I decided to give the T.C.C.B. XI a talk about teamwork and togetherness.

"Let's all get together in the dressing room at 10.30 for a chat," I said to the players as we were changing for practice. I thought I detected one or two smiles. Perhaps they knew what was coming.

I was nervous before I spoke and still unsure of what I was going to say. The players sat about in various stages of undress and were probably agitated themselves, as I had not yet tossed up. The chairman of the selectors, Alec Bedser, sat in a corner with fellow selector, Charlie Elliott. It was a daunting prospect.

"I know it's an unusual game and that we're all out to impress and show what we can do," I began. "But to be successful we will need to support each other, form partnerships and share experiences. That way we'll do even better for ourselves."

What a load of rot, I thought, as I spoke these words. We weren't 'in it' together at all; we were in it entirely for ourselves. It was quite simply an opportunity to impress the selectors, not to show what a great team we were.

Fortunately I wasn't put off by talking gibberish. Far from it. I persevered.

"So, although we've only just assembled today, let's approach this match as a unit working together and helping each other to perform even better. Let's have some fun in the process and enjoy the occasion. That's the way to succeed."

The longer I went on the less convincing I sounded, and this was supposed to be a great speech to rally the troops and impress the selectors.

That it was complete drivel could not be questioned, but I knew that it was not the content of the talk that mattered so much as the manner of its delivery. I was giving it plenty of enthusiasm, energy and passion to mask and camouflage the lack of substance.

"Right then, let's go for it, let's give 'em all we've got, and show 'em what we can do."

I was reaching a crescendo.

"There's heaps of talent here, let's not hold back, we'll give the opposition a hard time. Nothing to fear from them, medium pace and spinners and a lot of shot makers."

By this point, I was running out of steam and beginning to pace about.

"Good luck everyone, all the best, have fun and we'll see where we've got to by this evening. Time to toss up, I think."

And on that dynamic note I opened the door to my left, through which I planned to make my departure, and walked straight into the airing cupboard. This brought the house down and turned a lamentable performance into a memorable one.

Bedser and Elliott remained in their corner, looking startled. Who *had* they selected?

I closed the airing cupboard door as firmly as I could, trying to regain some sense of adult dignity, and made my way onto the ground where I won the toss and elected to bat. This decision, at least, was well-received, particularly by the bowlers who fancied a day with their feet up.

The match, which was played for the most part in gloomy, muggy and overcast conditions and watched by almost nobody, made well-disguised progress for two and a half days. The T.C.C.B. XI performed well. Everyone had had a chance to impress, and most had done so. But nothing of great interest happened until the last afternoon when I took Sri Lanka by surprise and declared, setting them a target of 197 runs in three hours. In the conditions and given a short leg-side boundary, I could not have been more hospitable.

The tourists did not like the look of it. They smelt a rat. They were caught betwixt and between. On the one hand they would instinctively chase this absurdly easy target, but on the other they could scarcely afford to lose a prestigious fixture just before their application for Test match status was to be heard. The dilemma became all the more apparent as their second innings progressed. Against some excellent pace and spin bowling Sri Lanka stumbled to 116 for five, and it actually looked as if we might bowl them out.

The rotund figure of Duleep Mendis was the last remaining recognised batsman. He was a tea taster from Colombo with, as I had discovered on the Thursday night, a taste for whisky, too. I knew also that he was a naturally attacking batsman, remembering how two years earlier at Horsham he had spoilt Geoff Arnold's afternoon by running down the pitch and flaying him through mid-wicket. Arnold's language was rich and based around the expletive "you curry-muncher".

Yet here was Mendis at Nottingham, uncharacteristically blocking every ball and not doing a very good job of it. He probably felt it was his duty to save the game. National honour depended on it. But such ungainly defensive play certainly made for dire cricket.

I was fielding at slip and also keen to make a mark.

"Why don't you play your natural game?" I suggested to him.

Mendis thought a second.

"Your fielders are too deep for me to do that."

"Why don't you put the fielders where you want?" I replied, realising that these were unorthodox tactics.

"Are you sure?" he said with an air of distrust.

"Quite sure."

So Mendis set the field. He brought in the mid-wicket, moved mid-on round a bit and adjusted extra cover.

Emburey, the bowler, was dumbfounded by these goings-on.

"Are we still taking this match seriously?" he asked.

I explained to Emburey that I wanted to invite Mendis to play his shots, which he was prepared to do if we brought the field in a bit.

"Why don't you toss it up too," I suggested, "to encourage him?"

John muttered something under his breath – I think it was about captains – and went back to his mark.

The tactics worked. Mendis began to play with much more confidence. He danced down the pitch to Emburey and hit him into the vacant mid-wicket area. Emburey looked astonished. He was not used to such rough and rugged treatment. Mendis quickly warmed to the task, and the turning point came when he clouted Emburey for three fours and a six in one over.

Not for the first time I had got carried away by my own enthusiasm and, by the time I tried to regain control and set the fields myself, it was too late. The match was beyond repair.

But what really miffed Emburey was that I brought myself on to bowl at the other end from him and immediately posted men around the boundary, particularly protecting the deep mid-wicket area. I proceeded to bowl rather fast and unambitiously, not joining in the fun at all.

"Typical," jested Emburey. "So much for the team talk. 'We're all in it together' and all that sharing crap."

Although we've laughed about it ever since, I've never been allowed to forget those two hours. Mendis, our tea-tasting, whisky-drinking friend from Colombo, was unstoppable. Despite losing seven wickets, Sri Lanka won the game with three overs to spare and, I have to admit, I felt a strange satisfaction in the result.

There was a pitch invasion at the end. A solitary Sri Lankan, waving his country's flag, raced onto the field, all smiles and joy, and embraced Mendis by trying to wrap his arms around him. No easy task.

"You are a hero," I told Mendis as we left the field in the dingy light. "The lines will be buzzing in Colombo."

As I passed the Sri Lankan dressing room, their manager rushed out and flung his arms around me, taking me by surprise and knocking me off balance.

"Oh thank you, thank you," he gasped, quite overcome with emotion. "You have done a great thing for Sri Lankan cricket. You should be granted the freedom of Colombo, I tell you. We are so grateful."

Never had I been so popular after losing a game. Even my own team – except Emburey, of course – thought it was rather fun. A few days later the Sri Lankans, while they were still in England, *were* granted the official Test status they so much desired and indeed deserved.

115

1981 was a remarkable year for Sussex. Above all, my belief in the players remained undiminished as the summer unfolded and they in turn warmed to my enthusiasm and eccentricity. I like to think that my style of leadership was uncomplicated and revolved around mutual trust, individual responsibility and a smile.

Winning matches in three days was no easy matter; always a mad rush. Twenty wickets had to be taken, and play would become progressively more frantic. Yet still we kept on winning. In the final month I believed we were invincible and could do no wrong but, in the end, it wasn't quite enough. By just two points we failed to reach our ultimate goal of winning the championship. I have come to realise that neither success nor disappointment give much lasting warmth, but the failure of that summer was a blow which from time to time would leap at me from out of the dark, seeking to plague me.

Strangely by the time the season ended and we had failed in our mission to win the championship, I was not feeling well. I had become bad-tempered and angry and felt downhearted despite the euphoria of the summer. My mind was racing; I was rushing at things. Even a day's fishing became an ordeal.

For some reason life's pleasures were diminishing; the future became clouded by fear.

14

THE SYDNEY CLINIC

Depression, Manic Depression, Bipolar Disorder, Nervous Breakdown. They all describe, not very well, a sensitivity of mind with which, for as long as I can remember, I have been closely associated. 'The enemy,' I call them, always lurking on the horizon but held at bay by therapeutic drugs which rebalance the chemistry of the brain and its complicated wiring.

In September 1981 Mary-Lou and I, together with Georgie, left England for a second winter in Sydney, where again I was going to captain the Grade side Waverley. I was disappointed that Sussex had only finished second in the county championship, but already I was starting to think how we might go one better the following year. England had defeated Australia and, with Mike Brearley retiring a second time from the captaincy, there were even one or two who were putting my name about as a possible successor.

Yet within two months I was confined to a clinic for the bewildered, depressed and sad in the eastern suburbs of Sydney.

It was during a limited-over fixture against neighbouring Bankstown that I came to a grinding halt. We batted first and made a reasonable total to which I assume, due to my lack of recall, my contribution was scanty. But it was in the field that my control on the game fell apart somewhat. Now this can happen to any captain even in the best of health and indeed frequently does. Players get littered about the outfield – as Vic Cannings used to say, like confetti at a wedding – and bowling changes become erratic and confused. I found that I simply couldn't remember anybody's name and, even worse, shouted orders to fielders using a string of names which didn't relate to any of them. Amidst the chaos I continued to bowl somewhat wildly from one end and to little avail while my colleague David Hourn bowled chinamen and googlies into the rough I was creating. A cunning plan but it didn't work, and Bankstown emerged triumphant.

There is unfortunately nothing unusual about a captain making a mess of a one-day match. It happens all the time. There are no bandages, no splints or plasters, not even a high temperature; mental instability can be rather disappointing and certainly not as glamorous as many other afflictions.

One of the problems with mental illnesses is that they frequently go unnoticed. I think I fell into that category. Despite my field placing nobody actually thought I had a screw loose. Yet within twenty-four hours Mary-Lou had called the doctor over and I was posted off to what I took to be a private clinic somewhere near the sea and not far from where we lived. It was a low moment.

What struck me first about this hospital was how normal everybody seemed to be, and for a while I wondered whether I was at the right address. There were one or two not unattractive girls, very thin, whom I took to be suffering from eating disorders and lack of nourishment. In the normal course of events I might even have been tempted to glance in their direction, but one of the many side effects of depression is that the opposite sex and any associated mild attraction are temporarily lost. Interest in most things went out of the window, especially sex and cricket.

I made very few friends, only one that I can remember. He was a small chap, quite young, called Dave. I never worked out what his problem was, and didn't like to ask. I wondered whether he might be a jockey. He was the right sort of size and had those funny legs with knees pointing outwards which suggest many hours spent in the saddle. Perhaps he kept falling off and had lost his nerve although I wasn't sure he looked bruised and battered enough for that.

Dave joined me every morning for breakfast. This was a ghastly meal and hardly designed to prolong the will to live. We were all made to get up for it, which we did, dragging ourselves down to the dining room in dressing-gowns and pyjamas. No one cared about appearance and nobody spoke. We queued up at the canteen where all manner of goodies were on offer, but very little got eaten. I sometimes had a go at the poached eggs but rarely did I eat them.

Their baleful eyes would stare up at me from the plate. Dave never said a word. Every now and then one of the girls would sit with us and at least looked ill enough to convince me I was in the right place. Demons were never far from the surface. There was not the slightest spark of humour. I was haunted then by the famous two lines from the English Hymnal,

No goblin nor foul fiend
can daunt his spirit.

Goblins and fiends were poised in the traps waiting for the hare to fly past before giving chase. They were always there and prepared to pounce.

Breakfast was followed each day by an event which we had to attend and for which we had to dress: the Morning Meeting. This was presided over by members of the psychiatric nursing staff and not infrequently by a tough and solidly built Australian lady called Jan. She was the leader of the group to which I was assigned.

Jan was fantastic. Her language was a bit rough but, if she had been any good at cricket, I would have had her in my team. Despite the best efforts of the nursing staff, most morning meetings were unproductive. Nobody much wanted to talk to a large group and besides, assuming that most of the patients were suffering from some sort of depressive illness, the mornings found most sufferers at their worst, displaying their symptoms more prominently. Things tended to pick up a bit as the day went on.

Much of the time I was bored. There wasn't much to do and, by and large, few patients felt like any activity. But there was in the games room a table-tennis table on which we occasionally played 'ping-pong'. It had never been a game to which I was particularly attracted, but every now and then someone persuaded me to have a go. On one occasion it was Lisa who asked me to play. Although she was in my group therapy class, she was not a girl I knew much about except that I gathered through listening to others that she was prone to fearsome fits of rather violent temper. She was a pretty girl but one with whom I had hardly ever entered into any form of conversation.

My instinct was that I had to play a canny game. She wasn't a bad player, but I could at least just about hold my own. I could tell she was competitive and very much wanted to win; after all, she was Australian. We traded shots quite successfully and the score reached 18-17 in her favour and a change of service. Although the bell for supper was due to ring at any minute, she then, without any provocation from me, said a very surprising thing: "Would you like me to show you my left nipple?" Despite being in a fragile state of health myself, I realised that I had to think quickly. To say 'yes' might imply that I actually was keen to see that relatively private part of her body, which I was not, despite its potential attraction in the right circumstances. To say 'no' threatened me with the hideous possibility of having to cope with a major tantrum, which I didn't feel able to deal with at this stage.

I could see that I was being put in an impossible position, part of my rehabilitation programme maybe. I tried to play for time and suggested that, with supper almost ready, perhaps now was not the best moment. "Why not finish the game," I said, "and then give this a bit of thought over the meal?"

The bell for supper rang. Bats and ball were rested on the table, and we made our way downstairs. Mercifully there was no more talk of nipples. It had been a narrow squeak, and I took my encounter with Lisa to indicate that I was on the road to recovery and clearer thinking.

While this was going on in the games room life was far from dull for Mary-Lou and Georgina back in the land of normality. Travelling back from supper with friends one evening they were rammed aggressively in the boot by a car accelerating out of control on the flyover at Bondi Junction. Such was the force of the collision that Georgina, strapped into a car seat in the back, propelled her dummy, which she was sucking at the time, with such power that it hit the front windscreen like a cork exploding from a fizzed up bottle of champagne. When Mary-Lou plucked up her courage from the drivers' seat and looked over her shoulder, all she could see was a wide toothless grin on Georgina's face. Completely happy she clearly thought the whole thing was a bit of a laugh and hoped it would happen again. Paul Parker, who was also out in Sydney at the time playing cricket for Waverley, somehow received a message and was extracted from his flat in Bondi by the news that Mary-Lou had collided with a drunk Australian driver. Paul came to the rescue and relieved Mary-Lou's shoulders of the burden of worry. The car, which was a crock anyway before the accident, was now in no condition to continue its life. It became clear after a little analysis that Mary-Lou had been at fault in that she had in fact pulled out sharply in front of the Australian. Fortunately her culpability was balanced by his alcoholic condition. So honours were even in the end. The news of the mishap was broken gently to me by Paul two days later for fear of disrupting my progress back to good health.

Not long afterwards, as was our custom from time to time, we the patients walked down to the sea for a swim before breakfast. The coastline was lovely – rock pools, sand and the sound of surf – which gave us an incentive to get up early. These excursions were quite popular and most of my little gang – Lisa, Dave and others – joined in. We would swim in the sea and then sun-bathe for a while on the rocks by way of drying off before returning to breakfast. On most occasions the girls would cast off their bikini tops so as to acquire a more even tan, including Lisa who showed no inhibition or anxiety at all about either of her nipples. Irritatingly she caught me looking, as I did not want to feel I had missed out on something I should know about. She cast me an angry look, grabbed her bikini top and strapped it on again. It's a wonder that psychiatrists manage to cope.

Although considered to be a model patient and not subject to bouts of violence, I did make several attempts to escape. There was nothing particularly heroic about these efforts – it wasn't exactly like tunnelling out of Colditz Castle – no, I would say a fond farewell at reception and simply walk out of the front door with the cheery smile of a man set free. When I got home, after a long uphill walk to our flat, I was not greeted with the joy you might have expected and, after a cup of tea, would be driven back without much ado and restored to my temporary sanctuary where I was told I had to serve my time.

Some time later I was indeed on the brink of being released from the clinic when I attended what turned out to be a final group therapy class with Jan. She was, on this occasion, challenging us, one by one, about our futures and how we were going to make our way in the world. When it came to my turn, I murmured something about cricket and family and playing for England, at which point thankfully she moved on.

Next was my friend Dave who was sitting beside me and Lisa on a sofa. "Now, Dave," Jan said. "Have you any plans for when you leave here?" There was quite a long silence, which was not an unusual thing in the sessions.

"Yes," he said, at last awakening from a trance. "I need to get my passport and papers prepared so that I can go and live in Denmark." I must say, I was bit surprised at this. Denmark seemed an awfully long way from Australia, and I wasn't sure about the horse racing potential either.

"Will you tell the group why you want to live in Denmark?" Jan continued, looking at Dave with cold eyes. There was another long and uncomfortable silence while Dave appeared to be summoning up the courage to tell us. After a long wait he confessed all: "My wish," he mumbled, "is to live somewhere where I can have sex with underage boys, and Denmark seems as good a place as anywhere."

I was completely dumbfounded. Such a thing had never occurred to me, even though I was well aware that Sydney was rather that way inclined. I found myself instinctively shuffling away from him on the sofa. This, in itself, was a hazardous procedure as it drew me closer to Lisa and, at this stage, I really hadn't got the energy for her to get the wrong idea. In fact, I need not have worried. The whole class was so stunned by Dave's appalling revelation that we all just sat there absorbed in our own thoughts, probably thanking our lucky stars that we were not similarly afflicted.

I suppose I learnt a lot from the Sydney experience. Jan was my hero. I also visited a Doctor Bartle from time to time, and he would talk to me very fast in Australian. The words flew from his mouth so rapidly that they had the same effect as a train accelerating down a railway line, rattling over the points and through several red lights and stations and bombarding my ears so violently that all understanding and sense were lost. How hard I found it to gather my wits and produce suitable responses when depression had taken such a firm hold. I didn't get the gist of what he was saying at all, but his voice and manner had an hypnotic effect and I usually felt better for my visits to him. He had the wisdom to reintroduce me to the drug Lithium, which I should have been taking all along, and, together with a strange mixture of anti-depressants, I gradually began to get better.

Just before Christmas I was ready to return home and really recover. But, unlike many other illnesses, depression has no discernable timetable from which comfort can be drawn. It's always a threat, simmering dangerously but out of sight, like a dormant volcano.

My greatest fear was that people in the cricket world should know about this disability or flaw. One or two people did get to hear and were very supportive, and yet I still wanted to cover up and conceal the reality of the illness and the stigma attached to it. Glandular fever, a good all-rounder, came to my rescue and for some time became a constant ally. I found that parts of this illness could be used to conceal the truth. It was not a condition that gave rise to too many questions or too much attention but was serious enough to attract a good measure of sympathy. That was a help. And the best thing about this new-found friend was that it recurred whenever you needed it to.

Now, years on, I think, why can't we all be a bit more open about the delicate affairs of the mind? It's a complex business, I know, and one which should command our fullest attention and understanding. I believe that the subtle dividing line between sanity and insanity is as narrow as that line which separates success from failure. Even now not enough consideration is given to getting the balance right.

And so a very dark and dingy chapter began to close. It had been an exhausting episode. Strangely enough there is an intensely physical side to both depression and mania, horrible feelings in the arms and legs that usher in despair and hopelessness. There was no doubt that the balance and perspective of life had temporarily deserted me; it seemed that every high point was countered by a low one, my mood careering from one extreme to the other. The emotion that superseded all was that of fear, an indescribable terror of the future and what it had in store.

Now, years later and middle-aged, I find myself thinking, 'Why be ashamed of something beyond control?' The perception and treatment of this illness is quite different from what it was and far removed from *One flew over the cuckoo's nest*. The time has come for us all to recognise that the fitness and strength of the mind is every bit as important as that of the body.

15

TWO SUMMERS, FIVE MEMORIES

Lord's, 1 June 1982

Nobody looked forward to the traditional May bank holiday fixture between Sussex and Middlesex more than Imran Khan. He loved Lord's. It was a spiritual home to him, and he liked to do well there. He lived not far away in Kensington and regularly used its nets and indoor school for practice.

In the 1982 match Sussex were involved in a run chase. Set 262 to win by Brearley on the last afternoon, Imran was pacing about anxiously in the dressing room, awaiting his turn to bat and discussing the game nervously with his friend and fellow overseas player, Garth Le Roux. "Shall I hook Daniel or duck?" he kept saying. "Garth, what shall I do?" He often turned to Le Roux for advice. He could not decide how to play the big West Indian fast bowler.

Le Roux and Imran had been inseparable since coming together at Sussex. Although quite different temperamentally, they were well suited in many ways. They shared rooms, travelled in the same car and often went out on the town together. It was a happy marriage.

Le Roux was lying on his back in the huge Lord's dressing room, reading a Wilbur Smith novel, while Imran posed this taxing question again. "What do you think, Garth, shall I hook or duck?"

He was swinging his bat about aggressively when Garth replied. "Don't be silly, man, duck it, of course."

"Why?" asked Imran.

"Because whenever you hook you're done for. You always get out."

Imran had no answer to this and in any case he was spared from replying because Sussex at that point lost another wicket and he was in. Down the flights of stairs he went, through the Long Room and out onto the field. The Sussex score was an unpromising 49 for three.

Imran joined Parker at the crease, and for a while all went well against Emburey and Edmonds, the best pair of spinners in the country at the time.

Imran played himself in sensibly, and it was not long before he was into his stride and beginning to bat with some comfort. The tea interval was fast approaching and the score had moved on to 100 when Brearley, who was directing things quietly from slip, suddenly clapped his hands and signalled to Daniel that he wanted him to loosen up for a spell. It was a strange decision because there appeared to be time only for one more over before tea. Daniel would need to get ready quickly. Be that as it may, Brearley had made up his mind to exchange spin for pace at the Nursery end, albeit for just an over. Daniel meanwhile put himself through a series of contorted exercises in preparation for his brief pre-tea blast at Sussex.

The moment came, and Imran was facing the bowling. Brearley made a lot of fuss about setting the field and meticulously placed two men, his best fielders, Butcher and Barlow, in the deep on the legside boundary. Imran eyed them suspiciously. "Shall I hook or shall I duck?" This perplexing problem was clearly still occupying his thoughts. For three balls Daniel pitched the ball up, and Imran played serenely forward; he looked perfectly at ease.

At about this time our twelfth man wheeled a large trolley into the dressing room laden with sandwiches, cakes and a huge pot of tea. The hungry players, diverted by the prospect of food, took their minds off the cricket for a moment and made a bee-line for the best sandwiches. Cricketers are scavengers at heart.

By now Daniel was running in to bowl again at Imran. Predictably, he banged the ball in short. Imran, despite his best intentions, could not resist the bait and, like a big fish, grabbed it. The ball was onto him a shade quicker than he thought; his head rocked back as he made contact and the ball spiralled high into the air towards those fielders on the legside boundary.

Imran cried "Oh no," as he set off for an optimistic single, passing Parker on the way. Meanwhile Butcher placed himself carefully beneath the ball and caught the catch. Imran out for 40 and Sussex 100 for four. Tea time.

Now there was a hush in the dressing room as the team prepared itself for what would be an uneasy period of mourning. Players grabbed their sandwiches and slunk off quietly into the background not wishing to draw attention to themselves. I, by now a captain of some experience, kept a low profile too. It was left to the twelfth man to handle the crisis. With heavy hearts, we patiently awaited Imran's return.

After what seemed like an age the door was eventually pushed open, and the two batsmen came in. They were greeted by respectful silence, only broken by the wretched twelfth man clumsily trying to pour out tea into the cups. This period of self-inflicted grief had to be shared by the whole team while Imran sat with his head in gloved hands, whispering over and over again, "No, no." He was inconsolable, and I was left wondering from my corner how to break this spell of gloom and despondency before the after-tea session began.

At this point, Le Roux, who had not yet looked up from his Wilbur Smith, came to the rescue. He lifted his eyes and, staring coldly at his friend Imran, he shook his head knowingly and in his harsh South African tone said, "Immy, our government might be right, you blacks will never learn."

They looked at each other for a moment and then Le Roux returned to his book. Nobody spoke. Quelled as it were by the presence of death and numbed by Le Roux's shocking remark, we watched Imran whose face, gradually but perceptibly, began to break into a sheepish grin, followed by laughter. The ice was broken; the crisis had passed; the funeral was over. "But I thought it was just right for hooking," Imran said in vain.

But no one was listening, and Le Roux continued to read his book. The dressing room was tranquil again and, although we proceeded to lose the match quite comfortably, we were at least back in the land of the living.

Derby & Taunton, June 1982

For whatever reason we had never been much good in the Benson and Hedges Cup competition, so it did come as something of a surprise to be driving up the motorway to Derby to play in the quarter finals.

Why on earth we were quite so bad, I can't imagine because in the past we had always done rather well in the Gillette Cup, whose rules were not dissimilar. It was a mystery. Perhaps Sussex cricket didn't come into its own until later in the season.

Despite this dismal track record we had in 1982 progressed beyond the qualifying rounds and were determined to make the most of it. Derby, it had to be admitted, was not an inspiring ground, laid out as it was on the old racecourse a little outside the town. Bleak and windy, it was also almost empty when we arrived save for the two umpires who stooped over the turf and gingerly prodded the damper patches. One of them was Dickie Bird.

"Hello Dickie," I shouted from the boundary's edge. "How are you?"

Dickie turned round with a jump when he heard my voice and began to walk towards me.

"Oh, there you are," he answered. "Couldn't think where the voice was coming from. I'm better, thank you, much better. Completely recovered, in fact."

"Oh dear," I said. "I didn't realise you'd not been well. What's been the matter?"

"Terrible business, terrible business, didn't you hear? I got hit, I did, I got hit." Dickie's voice rose an octave as he pointed to the place on his jaw where he had recently been felled.

"Dear, oh dear," I said again. "Who would do a thing like that? What happened?"

"It was Clive Rice who did it. Hit the ball back ever so hard; it cannoned off his partner and landed smack on the jaw here." He pointed to the spot again. "Knocked me clean out for over a minute. Very nasty. Could have killed me."

"Well, I never," I said. "Never knew we played such a dangerous game, risking life and limb, but you're all right now are you, Dickie?"

"Oh yes, I'm fine, fine, just a little shaken."

Poor old Dickie, taking the full force of a Clive Rice drive on the chin. That was no laughing matter.

The match was a dull one as one-day matches go. Played on a slow pitch, it was dominated by the bowlers, and we restricted Derbyshire to a modest score of 190. Back in the dressing room we were trying to work out some tactics with which to tackle the task. The solution came when Imran unexpectedly announced that he would very much like to open the batting.

"My temperament is suited to it," he said.

For want of any better suggestions I concurred. It was a surprising decision with little solid evidence to back it up. Call it a 'hunch'. Perhaps, I thought, that Imran might take as much advantage of the new ball when batting as he did when bowling.

The opening over was bowled by Steve Oldham to Imran, the third ball of which swung a little, and Imran edged it comfortably to Miller at slip. Another failed experiment. Imran shook his head when he returned to the dressing room and said quite simply, "Johnny, that was not a very good idea." I didn't have the heart to disagree.

But, by hook or by crook and despite this questionable batting strategy, we were steered to victory by a fine innings from Paul Parker and onwards to a place in the semi-finals; it was uncharted territory for Sussex.

Imran bade us farewell after the game. He was off to captain Pakistan. "You'll miss me," he said. I nodded my head but still thought it was a strange comment for him to make at the time.

"What, not enough rooms?" I said heatedly to the large foreign lady as I leant over the reception desk in the hallway of the Heatherton Grange Hotel near Taunton. We were supposed to be booked in there for the night before our Benson and Hedges semi-final against Somerset. Something had gone wrong.

"Just as I say, not enough rooms for all of you. You bring too many people," said the large lady.

She was right, of course. Our squad had multiplied due to injury worries, and now they had nowhere to stay. It was already late; music could be heard coming from the basement where clearly a party was in progress, and I was tired.

"What do you think?" I asked Garth Le Roux, my travelling companion. He merely shrugged his shoulders, sloped off unhelpfully in the direction of the music and disappeared. The problem was mine.

As I stood there, still leaning over the reception desk and staring at the ample cleavage of the large lady standing behind it, I found I had shifted from a mood of simple resignation to one of total despair. I was desperately seeking inspiration when the large lady came to my rescue and made a helpful suggestion.

"I'll tell you what I'll do," she said, "I'll book them into the bed and breakfast in the next village. You go to bed now and I will give them directions when they arrive."

I could have hugged her and probably would have done had she been in reach. Problem solved. The music continued to throb its way through the hotel and I went off, much cheered, to find my room and settle down to a good night's sleep before the big day ahead.

When I eventually found my room and turned the key in the lock, I heard strange noises coming from within, which clearly indicated that I would not be spending the night alone. The light was turned off, and the deep rumbling sound suggested that whoever it was was deeply asleep and preparing as conscientiously as possible for the day ahead. I tiptoed over the threshold and tried to keep as quiet as possible. Despite my best efforts I stumbled over what I took to be a pair of shoes lying abandoned in the middle of the floor and then banged my knee painfully on a wall heater, which was well disguised and protruding ominously from beneath the window. I could hardly have broadcast my entry to the room more publicly and my companion, recognising this, sat bolt upright in bed and said with remarkable cheerfulness, "Hello skip." It was Ian Gould. "Sorry skip," he went on, "shortage of rooms, bit of a cock-up, thought you wouldn't mind." I assured him that I didn't. "If it's all the same to you, skip, I'm off back to sleep. See you in the morning." Without more ado Gould turned over and continued his interrupted slumber. Meanwhile I climbed into the other bed and tormented myself with the horrors of Richards, Botham and Garner, an uncomfortable mixture and not conducive to a good night's rest.

"Poacheddy eggs or scrambleddy," the large foreign lady, who by now I took to be Italian, announced loudly as she greeted me in the dining-room for breakfast. "No need to look so worried," she said. "I packed the late arrivals off to the bed and breakfast. They are fine."

Much relieved I plumped for poached eggs. Not that I wanted them. Will people ever realise, I thought, how hard it is to eat breakfast, let alone poached eggs, when confronted with the prospect of facing Garner in less than two hours. "You must have the good breakfast," she said. Sadly she was far too jolly for that hour of the morning. No-one felt hungry, and one by one the players slipped away from the breakfast tables and prepared to leave for Taunton where they would meet up with the rest of the team.

Our semi-final against Somerset was an unfair contest really. In boxing terms it might have been described as a mismatch. Imran was away with Pakistan; Parker had a stiff back and was lying on the floor at home, staring desperately at the ceiling; Pigott had poisoned his arm with fertiliser spread on the outfield at Hove; and I was suffering from lack of sleep. To be frank we were a hotchpotch of a team for this important match, played in front of a full house at Taunton, but to be reduced within forty minutes of the start to 20 for four would have proved a set-back to the most resilient of outfits which we certainly were not.

We never recovered. 110 all out was never going to be enough and, although we did dismiss Richards cheaply, the match was over by mid-afternoon and with it ended our most successful run ever in the Benson and Hedges Cup. As I said, we had never been much good at it.

La Manga, April 1983

It was lunchtime at a special meeting of the Professional Cricketers Association, held in September at the conclusion of the 1982 season. I grabbed a plate of food and sat myself down at a table next to Pat Pocock and several other Surrey players.

"Now, tell me," said Pocock. "What are you planning for next year's pre-season training?"

I thought for a moment and then shrugged my shoulders. "No, no plans at the moment," I replied unambitiously. "I expect we'll freeze to death at home as usual."

Now Pocock hadn't been Surrey's wily off-spinner for the last twenty years for nothing, so he now used all his experience and proceeded to lure me down the pitch with a cunning flighted delivery. "Wouldn't you like to spend some of April in the sun?" he asked.

This was a crafty question which expected, in fact almost demanded, the answer "Yes." I hesitated for a moment and then, in as non-committal a voice as possible, I admitted, "That would make a change." I instantly knew that I had been dragged further down the pitch.

"There's a place called La Manga. It's in Spain. Surrey are going there next year. Why don't you come too?" Pocock went on. He was now finding a bit of rhythm. A pre-season trip with Surrey was being proposed, not an attractive prospect, but still, I didn't like to disappoint Pocock such was his enthusiasm for this venture.

"Let me think about it," I said, playing for time and realising that I was now stranded halfway down the wicket and still nowhere near the pitch of the ball.

Lunch was brief, and we were quickly back into our meeting which gave me a chance to consider Pocock's suggestion. It had to be admitted, pre-season was always a headache. In 1981 we had spent a weekend away at a local hotel, an initiative which seemed ambitious at the time. In 1982 we had stayed at home as usual, so perhaps the time was right to branch out and fasten our seat belts, as it were, in preparation for a little pre-season sun and entertainment.

The following April we flew from Birmingham Airport to join the Surrey squad on the southern coast of Spain. The La Manga complex was one which favoured golf as its top priority, with tennis coming a close second. Cricket, while attractively presented amidst the palm trees, came a distant third. The idea was to lure British cricketers away from the pestilence of the English climate and to fly them, just two hours away, to the sun where they could play cricket, golf and tennis to their hearts' content. On the face of it the plan had its merits.

We were housed in a selection of white-washed villas which neatly lined the hillside, and I was woken on the first morning by the sound of feet trudging past my door. Although only 6.30 a.m. I was just able to make out through the curtains the shapes of the Surrey squad, up bright and early for a training session. Micky Stewart led the way and disturbed the peaceful atmosphere by shouting words of abuse and encouragement at the cricketers in equal measure. I sat up in bed and, in a moment of wild anxiety, wondered whether the Sussex team should be following this example rather than having a lie-in and lazy breakfast.

That was the problem. Living cheek by jowl with another team one was bound to compare programmes – the 'anything they could do, we ought to match' syndrome. So the week became very competitive as players vied with one another for superiority, with training exercises becoming increasingly severe and irksome as the week dragged on.

On the field of play – an intimate little ground flanked by golf courses and a driving range – the competition was no less great when we tackled a series of matches against Surrey. Even back in England I had never enjoyed these preliminary 'warm-ups', fearing that the opposition might poach one's best new ideas, if there were any. It seemed misguided to try out and show off any new strategies on one's opponents in a practice match – a bit of a waste, really. In La Manga I felt very exposed to the scrutiny of the opposition, both on and off the field.

The first match, a limited-over affair played on a bright green and virtually unused artificial pitch, began peacefully enough with the Surrey openers, Alan Butcher and Grahame Clinton, easing their way comfortably into the 1983 season beneath a bright blue Spanish sky, and taking advantage of a rough outfield to sharpen up their running between the wickets. After half an hour I brought myself on to bowl, as much as anything else to spare myself from any more fielding.

I began my spell rather well against Butcher whose natural inclination was to attack the ball whenever possible, and I extracted from him a series of ineffectual pushes from my first five balls. Eager as ever to bowl a maiden, I pushed the final delivery of the over through a little quicker. Butcher, far from subdued and keen to make his mark, nipped down the pitch and drove the ball back at me just inches off the ground. Taken by surprise I stooped quickly to make the catch and, as I grabbed at the ball, felt a searing pain in my left thumb as the ball struck it before coming to rest on the ground in front of me. On careful inspection my thumb, instead of pointing forwards as it had been, was now aiming ominously towards Greig fielding in the covers. It was clearly the end of my day's cricket, a maiden over being my only consolation.

After a lengthy wait at the local clinic it was confirmed that the thumb was dislocated – probably chipped – bruised and generally damaged. It was bandaged up and I was firmly told, "No more cricket or golf for at least a week." By the time we were ready to leave the surgery, it was well into the afternoon and we were just on the point of departure when Gehan Mendis, our opening batsman, hobbled in.

I looked at him is despair. "Oh no, tell me the worst," I said. It transpired that, in attempting a quick single, he had slipped off the matting pitch and turned his ankle over. Disaster and agony. So he was now following in my footsteps to listen to the verdict of a Spanish doctor who must have been surprised to have his routine interrupted by a succession of cricketing injuries. Mendis was considered lucky. Although he had not broken his ankle, he had damaged the ligaments and the injury was deemed serious enough for him to take the next available flight home and receive treatment in England. Given the sequence of events so far I was rather envious but felt it my duty to stay and oversee the programme, albeit from the boundary.

I think what disappointed me most about the whole episode was that I couldn't even play golf, couldn't grip the clubs. This was a pity because at La Manga there were three magnificent courses to choose from and, in the Sussex versus Surrey golf tournament, I could do no more than caddy for Tony Pigott, supposedly our strongest player, who, strange though it may seem, was fit to play golf, which he did continuously, but whose back injury prevented him from playing cricket. Some might say that his was the perfect holiday.

As the week wore on, I became progressively more grumpy. I needed some light relief. By the penultimate day of our visit I thought it was time to try out my thumb by doing a little batting in the nets behind the pavilion where I could practise with the minimum of fuss or show. I asked a young player, Jerry Heath, to throw a few gentle lobs to me, nothing too demanding. We had just started when I saw, ambling over from the back of the pavilion, the large and forbidding figure of Surrey's fast opening bowler and overseas player, Sylvester Clarke. He had a ball in his hand and wandered up to the net where we were practising.

"Can I have a bowl?" he asked innocently enough.

I hesitated, playing for time while I thought as quickly as I could. If I turned the offer down, it might look as if I was scared (which I was, because Clarke was just about the fastest and most fearsome bowler on the circuit) and I didn't want to give him that impression as we had to play Surrey at least three times during the forthcoming season.

"Oh all right, but not too fast," I replied, trying to avert a tremor in my voice. Clarke proceeded to bowl at me off four paces. His idea of not too fast differed sharply from mine. Pain shot up my arm every time I hit the ball. Heath looked on with interest but could scarcely conceal his amusement while I tried to convince Clarke that I was neither scared nor inept.

Taking everything into consideration, not least Pocock's initial enthusiasm for the venture, I could not find it in my heart to feel that our first pre-season overseas trip, while enormously well-intentioned, was the success it should have been. For what it's worth neither Sussex nor Surrey had particularly distinguished seasons. Perhaps the English climate and home territory have their merits after all.

Taunton, May 1983

Success, when it did come, tended to come somewhat out of the blue and without warning. Such was the case when we visited Taunton in late May 1983, with the season by now well into its swing. Somerset were one of the most charismatic teams in the country and contained Botham, Richards and Garner; they had built a formidable reputation, particularly in one-day cricket.

Fortunately it was a three-day county championship game and Sussex, after being put into bat first, made an unexpectedly successful start. Everyone made runs: Parker 79, Mendis 65, Colin Wells 63, Alan Wells 61, Greig 59, Gould 33 and even I scored 26. How good it was to make a contribution and play a part in this feast of runs, 408 for six declared. Now all we had to do was to bowl out our opponents twice to win the match.

In the first innings we got rid of Viv Richards early and were making good headway until Denning came in to join Roebuck.

Roebuck was a stubborn fellow to get out and had come in to bat, curiously wearing a helmet with only one side-piece attached. His right ear was left unprotected.

Roebuck's reputation as an academic of sound thinking (he scored a first at Cambridge in law) led us and many other astute county cricketers to believe that there was a subtle and cunning motive to this eccentric use of headgear. Indeed there were several players from other teams who copied his example, dangerously exposing an ear to the hard ball in the belief that it might have a beneficial effect upon their game. It subsequently transpired that Roebuck, for whom tidiness, despite a clear mind, had never been his strongest point, had merely lost his side piece amidst the muddle of his cricket case and so gone in to bat without it. Technique and strategy did not come into it. How easily we are influenced when it comes to fashion.

But back to the match. By the second day the pitch was beginning to take spin and so I had brought myself on to bowl to partner Chris Waller. Things were still going well for us – Somerset had reached 160 for six – when I proceeded to bowl a really outstandingly bad ball to Denning. It was one of those balls which, as soon as it had left my hand, I wanted to grab it back before it reached the batsman, but it was too late. The offending delivery landed, as it was always going to, halfway down the pitch outside Denning's off stump. I shouted a warning cry to Waller who was crouched close in at silly point, but it was too late; the damage was done, and Denning lay back and cracked the ball with all his might for what would have given him four runs, had not Waller been directly in the line of fire. He took the full brunt of the blow on his knee and collapsed unsurprisingly to the ground from where he was carefully picked up and carried to the pavilion.

There were now two major worries uppermost in my mind. The first was that I had been responsible for wounding, at least for the rest of the match, our most influential spin bowler and putting him on the sidelines. The second was that as captain I now had to shoulder the responsibility for leading the Sussex slow bowling attack – and we still had to get Richards out in the second innings.

Despite the injury to Waller, Somerset followed on 182 runs behind and were batting again on the second evening. Roebuck, still wearing his unusual helmet, got out early and so into the evening sunshine swaggered Viv Richards. In just fifteen minutes before play ended for the day he stroked his way to 30 runs and stood as a colossal threat for the day ahead.

I fretted over Richards all night and awoke, sweating and uncomfortable, in the early hours. I lay there in bed, tossing and turning as I puzzled over my field placing for the great man. Even in my dreams there never seemed to be enough fielders. By the morning I was exhausted and arrived at the ground both dispirited and with no clear idea of what best to do. So I did what I usually did in such unpromising circumstances; I asked the team what they thought.

Sitting on the large table in the middle of the dressing room, I looked at everyone. "Tactics for today, what do you think?"

For once the players were united in their views. Gould, acting as spokesman, said, "Skip, you should bowl."

I said, "Why me?"

"Because Viv's always been a bit weak against spin early on, more likely to make a mistake. And, as you've injured our only other spinner, you've got to be the man."

Gould came to the end of his little speech, which clearly had the full support of the team. So the strategy was decided upon. I would bowl. It was rubbish, of course, to suggest that Richards was weak against spin but this was clearly neither the time nor place to shirk responsibility. I gulped nervously and said without much conviction that I would do my best.

The moment had arrived. I paced out my run-up in preparation for bowling the first ball of the day to Richards. I looked up at the tower of St James' church peeping out above the small old-fashioned stand behind me and offered up a silent prayer in the hope that the Almighty would look sympathetically upon my predicament. Overnight I had set the field so often in my bedroom but now I hedged my bets and settled for a careful balance of attack and defence: two close fielders and the rest littered about the outfield, strategically placed to defend the boundaries.

I ran gently in to bowl and was just on the point of releasing the ball when I felt it slip in my fingers. This caused it, when I let go, to loop out a little higher that I intended. Richards, who must have been looking forward to his morning's batting as much as I was dreading bowling, advanced down the pitch, his eyes alight with anticipation, to greet this inviting morsel. At this point something totally unforeseen occurred that could perhaps only be explained by my earlier supplication encouraged by St James' church.

Richards, aiming a savage blow towards mid-wicket, took his eye off the ball for a moment and 'yorked' himself, the ball creeping through beneath his bat and going on to hit the middle stump. There was a moment of silence which could be put down to stunned shock and surprise. This was followed by rejoicing and much back-slapping and hand-shaking. So momentous was this event that Le Roux, who was one of the many players fielding in the deep and was not often taken with emotion, ran right across the ground, grinning from ear to ear.

"Johnny," he said when he finally reached me. "I think that's the equivalent of catching a twenty-pound salmon first cast."

Le Roux's joy was prompted more by relief than anything else. He now knew that he too would be spared a Richards onslaught and that our day henceforward would be much more peaceful, which indeed it was. The game was won by mid-afternoon, and there was still time for some fishing in the evening.

By 1983 Le Roux had become a compulsive fisherman and needed no encouragement to join me in my favourite pursuit wherever we were. As soon as victory had been completed at Taunton we packed up our things and hurried off to the Clatworthy reservoir, a picturesque trout fishery about twenty minutes away in the Brendon Hills. Late in the evening, with the light beginning to fade, Garth hooked a fine rainbow trout which I successfully landed.

Looking at the fish lying on the bank and bearing in mind our enormous catch netted that morning at Taunton, we concluded that it had been a very good day. If only it were ever thus.

Hove, June 1983

It was getting late when the telephone rang. My wife, Mary-Lou, answered the call and I could tell by the look on her face that the news was not good. "What?" she said. "Fallen out of a window? He must have been drunk."

She was talking to the Sussex coach, Stewart Storey, who was telling her that Ian Greig had fallen out of the sitting-room window of his first floor flat and badly twisted his knee. I grabbed the telephone. "Tell me the worst," I said. "How bad is he?"

"He locked himself out of the flat, tried to get through the window, slipped, landed in the garden, off to hospital and not going to play for a while for sure," Storey told me.

"Oh dear, oh dear. So who's going to play tomorrow against Somerset instead?" I asked.

"Well there's a young lad from Hong Kong, on the Lord's ground staff, who played in the second eleven at Southampton last week. He's called Reeve, Dermot Reeve. He bustles in and bowls quite usefully, bats a bit too and full of energy. I think he might be your sort of cricketer."

It was now nearly midnight and, as I had no better suggestions to make, I didn't even have to sleep on it. Reeve was selected to play against Somerset, a man whom I had never before set eyes upon.

The next morning, while I was knocking up in front of the pavilion, I bumped into Peter Roebuck and became engaged in a conversation which distracted us from the business in hand.

"Who's your player practising over there?" I said, pointing to a young cricketer hitting balls vigorously against the advertising boards.

Peter said, "I've no idea. He's one of yours, I think, not ours. You really ought to know your own players."

I explained about Greig's accident and said I assumed that he must be Dermot Reeve. "I'd better go and introduce myself," I said and hurried off to greet the fair-haired youngster who already looked very much at home.

"Hello," I said. "My name's John Barclay. I'm your captain, welcome to the team, and good luck."

I don't think I was quite what he was expecting. He looked at me inquisitively as I asked him about his cricket.

"What do you bowl?" I said.

"Well, I can bowl quite fast and swing it both ways," he answered frankly, if somewhat immodestly. I felt reassured. Confidence didn't appear to be a problem for him.

We fielded first and, within a few overs, Reeve was introduced into the attack, bowling into the wind from the sea end. He didn't exactly bowl fast, but he did indeed bustle in and swing the ball. In no time he had snapped up the wickets of Denning, Lloyds and Palmer. In fact I had great difficulty in taking him off, even when he appeared to be tiring. "Oh please let me have just one more over." It was an irresistible plea.

Dermot became a great favourite with my daughter, Georgina, then aged two and a half. He lived near us in Hove, and I would give him a lift each morning to the ground. She would wait by the big window in our front room for him to turn up, which he invariably did by walking with spectacular success on his hands, feet splayed high in the air. For Georgina this was truly wonderful. Had it not been for cricket, circus life would have suited Dermot very well.

The match itself was a surprisingly low-scoring affair and, with no Richards, Botham or Garner playing, a relatively peaceful one. Sussex replied to Somerset's score of 181 with a modest 178 of which I made 6 before running myself out. I remember being surprisingly angry with myself and, in a fit of childish pique, I thumped what I took to be a wooden railing with my bat as I returned to the pavilion. Unfortunately the fence was made of plastic and to my embarrassment the entire structure collapsed. My dismissal could hardly have been more publicly advertised. My humiliation was complete when in the afternoon I attempted to put the fence up again. In this mission I discovered yet another of my weak points and failed miserably despite receiving plenty of advice and even some help from the members.

Le Roux, almost single-handed, routed Somerset in their second innings in the course of which I was struck a brutal blow on my right hand. I was bowling to Jeremy Lloyds who was one of the only batsmen making any headway when he flat-batted a ball back at me with deceptive power. I was taken by surprise and stuck out my right hand which took the full force of the shot and in the process more or less took off the end joint of one of my fingers. The ball rebounded towards mid-off where it was almost caught. The poor old finger, despite lots of attention, never really recovered. It made no difference to the match. Somerset were bowled out for 112 and Sussex, in Reeve's first match, won comfortably, an outcome that had seemed most unlikely three days earlier.

16

HASTINGS

Not often does a county championship match stick in the memory. There are just so many of them and they tend to merge, somewhat blurred, one into another. The game between Sussex and Kent played at the Central Ground in Hastings at the end of June 1984 was a rare exception and could not easily have been matched for drama and excitement. It was a mysterious game, the course of which was hard to explain.

Hastings is, of course, no stranger to drama. Despite the eccentric nature of the town, it is the chief of the Cinque ports and was already a flourishing harbour when William of Normandy landed in 1066 along the coast at Pevensey. Long before William's arrival the Romans had moored their vessels in the ancient port, but eventually it had dried out and left behind a meadow beyond the reach of high tides. This low-lying and damp area, hundreds of years later, became the Hastings Central ground at Priory Meadow.

It was just a few miles from the Kent border, and Derek Underwood seemed to adopt the ground as his own, a perfect surface for his lethal skills. Back in 1964, as a 19-year-old, he took nine Sussex wickets for 28 runs, the best bowling figures of his career. Three years later he took seven wickets in each innings. Then in 1973, when he dismissed me for a pair, he took 13 wickets in the match – including eight for nine runs in the second innings.

Now the meadow is a shopping market. It is surrounded by all the trappings of the consumer world, with little indication of its history.

The weather for our 1984 match was fine. The pitch had a tinge of green, but no more, and Tavaré, the Kent captain, must have felt confident when he won the toss and elected to bat. By just after lunch Kent had been bowled out for 92 with only Taylor and Aslett reaching double figures and Colin Wells tearing the heart out of their innings with five for 25. Sussex didn't do much better, and the tiny Hastings dressing rooms were a hive of activity all day with batsmen falling over each other as they prepared to 'pad up' for action.

Before the day was over Sussex were dismissed for 143, a lead of only 51, and still there was time for Kent to lose a second innings wicket. This brought Underwood to the crease as a night-watchman to protect the established Kent batsmen.

When play resumed on Monday morning Kent once again collapsed against the might of the Sussex seamers, Le Roux, Reeve, Wells and Greig. That is, all except for Underwood. He played with serenity and control throughout the morning and on after lunch while all about him wickets were falling. The harder the bowlers tried, the more Underwood appeared to relish the challenge. He evaded bouncers by jumping out of the way, and the yorkers he stabbed out effectively at the last moment. For some reason the bowlers didn't bowl as well at Underwood as they had at the other batsmen. The cut and square drive were his most productive stokes. Soon after he had passed 50, I caught him at slip off a no-ball. I think that was as close as we ever got to getting him out.

Kent were struggling at 155 for eight, a lead of just over 100, when Alderman joined Underwood in a partnership that further tormented us. Alderman scored his maiden half-century and Underwood, at the age of 39, completed his first and only hundred in the 22nd season of his career and 618th first-class innings. As a result of these heroic performances Kent scrambled their way to 243 all out, a lead of 192. There was a day's cricket still remaining.

The sun shone and the gulls shrieked as we set out to tackle this modest target on the Tuesday morning. We began brightly enough against Jarvis and Ellison before Alderman was introduced into the attack and he, with Underwood, gradually began to subdue our spirits. This was not a dramatic collapse of the sort we were well used to but more a gradual subsidence. From a promising 39 for no wicket we slipped to 133 for six in now perfect batting conditions. It was a lamentable performance. The batsmen, myself included, all seemed to make a steady start, then get out.

Lunch came and went. Gradually Ian Greig and Colin Wells, the older of the two brothers, began to repair the damage while in the crowd a small gathering of faithful followers, slouched in their deck chairs, observed the proceedings with a watchful eye, picnics and flasks at the ready to sustain them.

As the partnership between Greig and Wells slowly took shape and the runs began to tick over, I grew increasingly fidgety and nervous. Believing that the captain, despite constant provocation, should always remain calm and free from agitation, I took myself off for a quiet stroll around the ground, leaving the players to fend for themselves in the pavilion.

Halfway round, I stopped to buy myself a cup of tea and, feeling a little more relaxed, sat down on one of the many spare seats to watch the cricket from a new vantage point. I had not been there long before I was joined by an old man in a long coat, a complete stranger, who came to sit beside me. I knew it was only a matter of time before he would engage me in conversation.

"You look tense and nervous," he said. Before I had time to answer he added, "Can I give you some advice which I have always found helpful in this sort of situation?"

I knew that, whatever I said, he was bound to continue.

"Years ago I used to coach high-jumping."

"Oh yes," I said, wondering what was coming next and

whether this was what I needed to help us through our plight.

"Do you know what I used to tell my young jumpers?"

I shook my head in resignation.

"I used to tell them to throw their hearts over the bar and that their bodies would automatically follow. It used to work wonders with athletes who were anxious or nervous. Tell that to the team."

By now I was beginning to take an interest in this strange old man who had appeared out of the blue. I finished my cup of tea and thanked him for his advice.

"Throw your heart over the bar."

Much comforted by the old man's words, I returned to the pavilion where spirits had been considerably lifted by Greig and Wells whose batting had taken us past 150; we were now within 40 runs of the target. They batted serenely on until, with the score 186 and with just seven more runs needed, Alderman had Wells taken at slip for a pugnacious 81.

The first ball of the next over Greig drove imperiously for four. It was 190 for seven and only three runs were now required with three wickets in hand. Off the next ball Greig attempted the winning hit but misjudged the length – and Potter took a high swirling catch, tumbling backwards at mid-off.

190 for eight. Three runs still needed.

In walked Le Roux, always a reliable man in a crisis. He pushed meekly forward to his first ball from Ellison and was caught at slip by Tavaré. 190 for nine.

Disaster. Still we needed three to win, two to tie. Our last man, reserve wicket-keeper David Smith, came to the crease without much form to go on.

Somehow or other he and Waller scrambled two singles to bring the scores level. Surely we could snatch another run from somewhere. But no, it was not to be. Alderman completed the match by angling a ball across the left-handed Smith. He edged it to Tavaré who caught yet another catch.

The match was tied. We had failed at the final hurdle. Perhaps if the old man's message had had time to get through and we had thrown our hearts over the bar, the result might have been different.

Setbacks such as these, even at the end of historic matches with honours even, are hard to cope with. Players are frustrated and deeply disappointed. Pride is hurt. Blame is handed out indiscriminately, and friendships take a back seat. Team spirit, that much heralded asset, takes a bashing. Invariably the captain, never blameless himself, is left to pick up the pieces for another day. I never found that easy.

17

THE AUSTRALIANS AT HOVE

It was 1985 and, in preparation for their Test series against England, Australia for the first time played a number of four-day matches against the counties, one of which was with Sussex in the middle of May. It was, I suppose, a forerunner to a four-day county championship although it was still eight years until that programme was fully implemented. While generally heralded a success, Sussex's match against Australia, despite building up into a gripping climax on the final day, was an uncomfortable encounter for me and one which I would rather forget.

For the first two days the game progressed quietly enough. Australia, with David Boon scoring a pugnacious hundred, batted on into the second day before eventually being bowled out for 321. Sussex's reply, while solid, was equally unspectacular and drifted into the morning of the third day which we started on 216 for eight.

Believe it or not, I was still batting and the score had risen to 258 for nine when Jeff Thomson, Australia's bowling hero of the 1970s, decided to take the new ball, a tactic to which Sussex, who rarely survived for so long, were wholly unaccustomed.

His first ball of the over was a 'loosener', a wide swinging full half-volley outside the off stump, at which I swung my bat with great gusto; I could recognise a scoring opportunity when I saw one. I made contact but only with the outside edge. The ball ballooned over the in-fielders and spun away to the boundary for four. "Jeez," somebody in the slips said. "Can't you do better than that, Thommo?"

Thomson was not amused and stared at me menacingly.

"Oh help," I thought as I prodded the pitch nervously. "I've annoyed him now."

Indeed I had. Thomson paced out his full run-up and prepared to bowl the next ball. This time his legs were pumping hard, his long mane of fair hair flowing out behind him as he accelerated into his powerful bowling action. As his arm came back in preparation for releasing the ball, I stood resolutely still, unflinching, determined to give away nothing of my apprehension.

Thomson's bowling arm swung through in a wide slingy arc. I heard the ball hit the pitch – I guessed somewhere nearer him than me – but failed to get a clear sight of it. Despite attempts to defend myself, the ball unfortunately collided with my face and, without showing any signs of bravery, I collapsed in a heap on the ground by the stumps. I was fully conscious throughout but felt it was wise to take my time and make the most of the drama.

Kepler Wessels was first to reach the battle scene. He was playing for Australia but was at least a friend and a former team mate with whom I had opened the batting for Sussex in the late seventies.

"Bad luck, Trout," he said to me, using my nickname, "but you've been batting long enough anyway. You might as well declare."

The other fielders and even Thomson himself had by now gathered round and everyone agreed that the suggestion had its merits.

"Good idea, Kepler," I said. I knew from old that Wessels hated fielding and the Australians had had enough of it, too. So my decision to declare was a popular one which found favour with the Australian team and even their fast bowler Thomson who, on his way off the field, took the trouble to autograph my bloodstained gloves. They made a lucrative auction item in my benefit year in 1986. It just goes to show that even minor setbacks can be turned to advantage.

When I reached the pavilion steps, I saw a friend waiting to greet me. His name was John Samways, a young curate from the parish of Patcham near Brighton. He had been introduced to me through an organisation called Christians in Sport and was now, I suppose, acting as a sort of unofficial chaplain to the team, in reality more of a friend and wise counsellor. Anyway, I had decided that he could only be good for the spiritual needs of Sussex and so he attended as many of our matches as possible. I was pleased to see him at the top of the steps today at this moment of discomfort.

"Bad luck, old man," he said, looking at me sympathetically. Since his arrival at Sussex I had frequently been asked what possible purpose an Anglican minister could serve for a cricket team and, in my painful predicament, was expecting him to show his true worth as a man well used to all the regimes of crisis. "What do you think then?" I muttered through my swollen jaw. He looked at me sadly and then said, "Well, if you had gone back a bit further and brought your hands up higher, I think you'd have played the ball a lot better." It was not a helpful comment.

Confident that no long-lasting damage had been inflicted upon my face, I drove myself across Brighton to the Royal Sussex County Hospital where I joined the long and depressing queue in casualty and patiently waited my turn. Eventually I was seen by a doctor who looked iller, or at least more exhausted, than any of his patients and possibly in greater need of treatment.

From there I was directed to a hospital dentist with whom an appointment was arranged that same afternoon. My teeth had been shaken up a bit by the force of the ball.

I joined another queue and, while I waited, wondered how

the match was progressing at Hove. Would they miss me a lot or even at all? I hoped so. "We can't do without you," I wanted to hear them say. "You're indispensable." But sadly it was never quite like that.

Some three hours later, with my gums stitched up and feeling a bit sore, I was released from hospital and drove back through the evening rush hour to the ground where Australia, with a first innings lead of 59, had been scoring some quick runs. I was keen to get back on the field as soon as possible and return to the thick of things. Indeed I planned to have a bowl myself. After all, I had bowled rather well, I thought, in the first innings and, despite the impending threat of Border and Boon at the crease, it seemed only right that I should have another go.

I peeled off my sweater, handed it to the umpire, David Evans, and paced out my short run-up. I was busy setting the field when I saw that Evans was becoming agitated and began to address me quite sternly.

"You can't bowl," he said.

"I'm sorry," I replied and asked him to repeat himself.

"You can't bowl," Evans said again, a little louder this time.

Many players and even friends had told me that in the past.

"No, you can't bowl," Evans explained. "You're not allowed to. You see, you've been off the field for more than two hours, and you can't bowl again until you have spent the same length of time on it."

"Oh dear," I said and apologised for the error and for the delay. I waved to Imran who, up until then, had found the incident highly entertaining. I asked him to come and bowl and, without so much as a grumble, he paced out his long run-up.

As I threw him the ball, I looked down the pitch at Border, shaping to take guard against Imran. I don't think I have ever seen such an undisguised expression of disappointment in a batsman's face.

The match ended happily enough with Imran and Le Roux batting out time on the final day against the leg-spin of Holland and off-spin of Matthews. Four-day cricket had arrived at Hove, but the tempo and style had changed very little.

18

LAST DAYS AS A CRICKETER

If anything had changed in Sussex cricket, it was a subtle shift in direction away from an emphasis upon first-class cricket, which so nearly brought the county championship to Hove in 1981, to a closer affinity with the one-day game. This was without doubt far more rewarding financially, even if socially and intellectually less demanding.

In the early eighties, on Sunday afternoons large crowds still flocked to watch what was then the shortest available match, 40 overs a side. For many years I had treated this form of cricket merely as a necessary chore which had to be performed as part of a professional contract. Perhaps I had become too much of a cricketing snob, but for me it rather spoilt the prospect of a day off, sandwiched as it was between the three days of a county championship match. It was mad, other than for the sake of much-needed cash, to expect cricketers to change gear so suddenly and maintain their enthusiasm and zest for what they were doing for the rest of the week.

But Sussex, more by luck than design, found a winning formula. It was based on confidence and its healthy side effects. In early 1982 we won our first few matches and this produced an irresistible momentum. In fact, we only stumbled once in all these Sunday matches, against Worcestershire at Horsham.

From a hopeless position, as shadows lengthened in the evening sunshine, John Inchmore, hardly a household name, altered the course of the match in favour of Worcestershire with some clever deflections to fine leg, which was left undefended as fielders were needed elsewhere. We lost the match and, sitting as we did in the dressing room afterwards trying to work out what had gone wrong, Imran Khan raised his voice.

You may remember he had once played for Worcestershire himself, and he said, "Old Inchers only has one shot; how foolish not to have had men defending the leg side boundary."

Ian Gould looked up from his corner and added dryly, "Bit late to tell us that now, Immy."

The matter was closed and, as it transpired, we didn't lose again all summer and won the Sunday league by defeating Middlesex in August in front of a large crowd at Hove and amidst much celebration. We scored a record number of points that year which, so far as I am aware, has never been bettered.

We were up with the leaders in 1983 and 1984, just falling away in the final straight, but in 1985, very much towards the tail end of my career, we came within a whisker of winning it again.

How this unfolded is less plain to me now than it was then. In the early games we played inconsistently and lost almost as many as we won. But by mid-July, when we travelled to Northampton, we were still just about in the hunt though we could ill-afford any more slip-ups.

It was a hot day and one on which my tactical skills were not at their sharpest. I miscalculated the overs the bowlers had bowled and found to my alarm that I was an over short at the end of the Northants innings. I had no option but to bowl it myself. Twelve runs were needed for a Northampton victory. David Wild and David Ripley were my immediate adversaries. Six balls to bowl and twelve runs to win, it was just like playing in the nets, but for real.

I bowled the first five balls as fast as I could. David Wild hit the first four for two runs each, mostly in the direction of the football ground where the surface was particularly bumpy. Garth Le Roux and Tony Pigott were patrolling the area and, by the sound of it, not enjoying their Sunday afternoon at all. Wild managed only a single off the fifth ball, and that left David Ripley on strike for the last ball.

I set the field with great care. It was two to tie and three to win. I bowled with sweaty hands and dry mouth. As I released the ball, I felt it slip just slightly in my fingers – I had intended to bowl a fast searching yorker – but, with control lost for a moment, the ball looped up temptingly outside Ripley's off stump. He was clearly taken by surprise and lifted his head in anticipation of glory; he played over the ball and was bowled.

As Ian Gould, our wicket-keeper, pulled up the stumps to signify the end of the match, he looked over to me and asked, "What was that, skip?" I shrugged my shoulders, smiled and walked off to have a well-earned drink.

Scarcely a month later, we set off for Taunton to play Somerset, still one of the most feared teams in one-day cricket, with Viv Richards and Joel Garner at the height of their powers. By now we were at the top of the table and another win would just about have sealed our triumph.

It was not to be. Chasing a modest Sussex score of 184, Somerset had already reached 88 for two when Richards came in to bat. Imran, who was sometimes better at giving advice than receiving it, trotted over to me from his fielding position. He suggested that Viv, if anything, was more vulnerable to spin than pace early on in his innings.

"You ought to have a bowl," he said. "It's worth a try."

I wasn't quite sure about this as we were for ever playing Somerset at Taunton, and I always seemed to be bowling at Richards. Bad planning. Anyway, I did as I was told and paced out my short run-up from the River Tone end.

I bowled just one over that afternoon. Two balls landed in the river, doubtless startling the Sunday afternoon fishermen and probably the fish too; one was nearly caught on the boundary but dropped over and the others I can't remember. Twenty-six runs came from the over, at the end of which Imran had the decency to wander over to me and say in as sympathetic tone as he could muster, "Johnny, I don't think that was a very good idea." It was briefly touching to find such humility in a man so renowned for self-confidence and high self-esteem.

Despite winning our final fixture against Glamorgan, we were pipped for the title by Essex. Although it had been fun to be in the hunt all season, I was fast coming to the conclusion that my time in professional cricket was nearly up. My energy and enthusiasm for the relentless demands of the fixture list were beginning to run out of steam.

19

ARUNDEL

Shortly before that match at Taunton in 1985, we had been playing against Kent at Canterbury during their traditional cricket week in August. It was perhaps one of the few occasions in the season when first-class cricket joined hands with Kentish society and, as a result, included a fair amount of grandeur and pomp. The Band of Brothers and I Zingari were prominent in the marquees, and the band played. It wasn't quite Lord's, but this was county cricket with a bit of a swish to it.

Unfortunately rain prevented any play on the first day. The cricket was quickly abandoned as indeed were the smart tents decorated in club colours. Pretty girls in fetching hats were scarce amidst the puddles, and small streams ran down the slope through the tables and chairs and flowed onwards towards Canterbury. There was no one to be seen except, I think, Jim Swanton who rather thought we should be playing despite the conditions.

Given all the evidence of damp, I concluded that it might be a fishing day. My father was staying nearby in Charing with a great wartime friend of his, Peter Wilkinson, who had access to some fishing on the Kentish Stour. With Garth Le Roux in the passenger seat, I drove with as much haste as possible on the slippery roads to the water's edge where we were greeted by the two second world war warriors. Supplies always being at the top of the agenda in the army, they had generously provided the picnic. But, what with the wind and the trees crouching and bending over the river, fishing was neither easy nor particularly pleasing. Extracting flies from branches is a frustrating business and not one which improves the mood.

Le Roux, a placid man in most circumstances, was clearly not enjoying himself as much as usual, an impression I got from frequent lapses into dressing-room language as he pulled aggressively at his line entangled in some hideous and prickly obstacle. As the rainwater began to run ominously down our necks, and backs, it was one of those occasions when we would have preferred to play cricket. Even the picnic was little compensation.

I did at least catch one small trout, but without doubt my father and Peter Wilkinson came out of the ordeal better than us young ones. I think we have to put that down to army training.

At Canterbury on the following day, with the sun now shining, the match took an unusual course. Sussex batted first and scored 317, not bad for us, and in reply Kent generously forfeited their first innings. After adding 27 more runs, Sussex declared and set Kent a target of 345 to win on the last day. Match-fixing in those days was not uncommon, but all in a good cause.

It was 10.55 a.m., and I was sitting in the dressing room at the St Lawrence ground, having a final cup of tea and considering our bowling options for the day ahead, when the telephone rang. It was one of those telephones which was stuck to the side of the wall and kept us in touch with the outside world. Colin Wells answered it. "Captain, it's for you. Colin Cowdrey."

It was an unusual time to get a call and particularly from a cricketing hero, one of the game's giants. With the umpires half way out to the pitch, brevity was of the essence.

"Arundel," Colin said. "Would you be interested in running a new project at Arundel Castle?"

With the rest of the team now going down the stairs and about to reach the outfield, I said, "Yes."

"I'll be in touch then," and Colin's voice faded away.

For months I thought little more about this brief encounter and was unaware of its significance. The Kent match came and went. We won it in the last over, bowled by Le Roux, when Kevin Jarvis, one of the world's most spectacularly bad batsmen, spooned me a catch at slip.

Since the fishing on the first day and grappling with all those bushes, Le Roux had somehow rid himself of those traits of grumpiness that so often mar a cricketer's life.

With the season finished and holidays over, I returned to my winter job. Since 1983 I had been working at six-monthly intervals for a company based in Brighton called International Factors, part of the Lloyds Bank group. I travelled around the country in support of its marketing department. My task, from time to time, was to host seminars and presentations. I had to jolly guests along and convince them of the benefits of financing businesses through the obscure world of factoring. Fortunately on these occasions I was only the front man. I was surrounded, thank goodness, by experts who would field awkward questions and speak with enthusiasm on the subject. I learnt a little about the business as time passed, just enough to get by, but my heart wasn't in it. Financial tools were never going to be my cup of tea. Profit didn't interest me and money even less. My cricket statistics alone prove that I was never a slave to greed.

Shortly after Christmas 1985, as I remember it, the telephone rang again.

"Colin Cowdrey here – come and have tea at the weekend."

So we did. Mary-Lou, Georgina (then aged almost 5) and me.

I was, of course, already very much aware of Arundel and its famous ground. Several times I had played there and in 1977 had even represented Lavinia, Duchess of Norfolk's XI against the Australians; rain set in after half an hour, shortly after I had got out.

I was also one of the original members of Lavinia's club which she called the Friends of Arundel Castle Cricket Club. This club she established in memory of her husband Bernard, who died in 1975. It would provide the means and heart by which cricket could continue at Arundel, but lack of money and support were problems that were never far from the surface. The cricket and the club were not exactly on their last legs, but there was clearly need for a further injection of life. Throughout the early eighties, it had become clear to Cowdrey and his great friend Roger Gibbs that there were generous people who loved Arundel and its heritage, but they would only consider giving tangible support if a charitable organisation could be born.

That is where I came in. With remarkable speed, an application was completed and sent to the charity commission, based upon the sound and strong criteria of 'youth and education'.

I needed little enticement to become the Director of Cricket and Coaching; thus the Arundel Castle Cricket Foundation started its life. It was immediately blessed with a magnificent contribution from the late Sir Paul Getty. His generosity got the new project off the ground and enabled us amongst other things to build a fine cricket school just behind the original pavilion.

The combination of the Friends and the newly formed charity gave cricket at Arundel renewed impetus. Nothing would be taken away from the traditional fixture card. Arundel would continue to provide a home for good club cricket and for cricketers not wishing to be enslaved by tough Saturday afternoon league cricket. Tourist and charity matches, so much a feature of Duke Bernard's cricketing years, continued to flourish.

In 1963, aged nine, I had visited Arundel for the first time with my grand-parents from Horsham to watch that great West Indian side play their opening match against the Duke's team. It was a fine day at the end of April, and I remember a huge crowd. We sat on the bank near the famous gap in the trees on the far side of the ground. Worrell the captain, Sobers, Nurse, Hall and Butcher played for the West Indies, and it seemed that the Duke had recruited more or less the whole England team: Barrington, Dexter, Cowdrey, Graveney, Titmus, Allen, Knight, Murray and even Alec Bedser to lend a little experience. The West Indies won the game, and for my part the day was a great success until on the journey home I got bitten on the nose by my grand-parents' poodle, Tessie. A surprising amount of blood gushed from my punctured nose; with my dignity battered, I have rarely looked upon poodles with affection since.

Amidst the history and heritage of Arundel, it took me a while to find my feet. It was hard to adjust from the cut and thrust of county cricket's strange world to the calm waters of Arundel's peaceful haven. For a while I was stunned by the silence and unsettled by the wintry darkness that removed me from the real world.

As it turned out, my transition from one existence to another did not last long. I was quickly into my stride and keen to learn all I could about the young and how cricket might help to develop their lives. Starting close to home, I visited a great many schools and established an extensive local programme amongst many young people who had never been introduced to the game before. They loved it and were surprised to find that cricket was not as dull as they had been led to believe.

I realised that this new project would make little impact if it did not include the inner cities and particularly those London boroughs where the young are frequently deprived of opportunity and progressively denied access to playing fields on which to run about. With the help of the London Community and London Schools Cricket Associations, I gradually made an impact upon an area where help was badly needed. My intention was to invite groups of children to Arundel and find somewhere for them to stay so that they could enjoy the wide open spaces and green grass of the countryside.

Since 1988 these trips have become a regular feature, and thousands of young Londoners have benefited from the experience and returned again and again. Above all, they are enchanted by the ground, the trees and views. The castle holds a fascination as does the seaside. A great many of our visitors have neither seen a castle nor been to the sea, let alone paddled in it.

As you might expect, there is no shortage of wildlife at Arundel, rabbits and pheasants being the most prolific species. Unsuccessful stalking has become a great pursuit for the children, not something that occurs readily in Hackney, Islington or Tower Hamlets. The odd fox may be seen. Rare birds have been known to put in an appearance too: a peregrine falcon, a sparrow hawk and, more recently, buzzards. A red kite is rumoured to have been spotted as well. Whatever else, it's a new world – exciting and stimulating for young impressionable minds.

When I started at Arundel, I saw the project through the eyes of a cricketer. I felt it as my mission, in the first place, to encourage the young to play the game and improve their performances through good coaching – commendable aims, I am sure. But the years have passed, and now I feel that our objectives at Arundel run a bit deeper. My thoughts and ideals centre more upon the individuals and their values in life than on the game itself.

In short, cricket has for me become the excuse or medium for youth development – and a very good medium it is, too.

The whole project took a giant step forward when the cricket school was completed towards the end of 1989. It is a magnificent building designed by Neil Holland, a distinguished local architect and built by Alan Wadey who since has become Chairman of the Friends and a trustee of the Foundation. Overnight, the scope of the operation expanded. No longer did we worry about the weather, and long dark winter nights held no fears. With a cricket ground and an indoor centre of such high quality, we now had the fundamental ingredients for success. As a result of this more than 250,000 young people have now taken part in our programme of activities and benefited from the experience.

One hot day in August 1991 and with the support of The Prince's Trust, HRH The Prince of Wales visited Arundel and gave his blessing to the project. Amidst much cricketing activity indoors and out he officially opened the cricket school, cut the ribbon and sportingly joined in the activities, being persuaded to play a game of cricket with the assembled children.

Prince Charles played his part with some style and chatted to all those who came into his path. This included one of my Rastafarian friends from Lambeth whose enthusiasm for cricket was matched only by the length of his dreadlocks. A lovely man he was and with a great zest for life and roll-your-own cigarettes. It was a stroke of bad luck that, when the Prince came up to him, he had just stuffed into his mouth a handful of potato crisps.

Prince Charles asked him about his work in Lambeth. The outcome of his question was not plain, but I doubt whether the Prince has ever been so liberally showered by half-eaten crisps when the answer came. Notwithstanding this minor setback, the day was a great success. Our programme, particularly amongst London children, got off to a powerful start from which it has never really looked back.

It was in these early years that Alex Tudor, who went on to play for England in the nineties, visited us as a schoolboy; long legs he had and he never stopped smiling. More recently Billy Godleman made his mark and has since established himself in the Middlesex team, with the potential of greater things to follow.

For the most part our aim at Arundel is not the unearthing of great talent; we tend to leave that to others. Our mission is to champion the cause of those for whom life is a real struggle. With this in mind we have in recent years established a programme for children with all sorts of special needs and disabilities. The blind and deaf have taken the field together, alongside those with a myriad of physical and mental problems. They all need encouragement, and they positively thrive on the attention they receive at Arundel.

The pressures on the young are enormous. What we are trying to do is to take the children away from their usual environment, for a brief moment, and to transport them into one which is not only safe and secure but also gives them the chance to taste something worthwhile and wholesome.

When Duke Henry in 1895 had the vision to carve a cricket ground out of the Sussex downland, he would not have anticipated its impact upon the game and society just over a hundred years later. Arundel Park, its beauty and stunning setting, has given pleasure to thousands, and we intend it to continue in that vein for many years to come.

20

FROM PROFESSIONAL TO AMATEUR

I can't deny that it came as something of a shock when in 1987, after nearly 16 years as a professional cricketer, I regained my amateur status and played cricket just for fun. I rediscovered many friends whom I had neither seen nor played with or against for years. Unlike many of the professionals I had been playing with, they still loved the game with a schoolboy passion; they didn't want it to rain and compensated for their weekday occupations with days spent in grassy outfields and tea between innings, a million miles away from any professional treadmill. Perhaps the main difference between the professional and the amateur is that the latter wants to play all the time and whatever the weather. Boyish enthusiasm had not been eroded by relentless analysis in county dressing rooms.

The amateur is essentially an ambitious volunteer who loves playing cricket and it was into this happy atmosphere that I was plunged in the late 1980s, but it did take me some time to adjust. Initially I felt exposed when I went out to bat, preferring to open if at all possible so as to avoid walking out on my own. I sensed I was a bit of a prize scalp and that the bowlers tried that much harder against me than the others. In truth, though, my heart wasn't really in it and, as often as not, I failed just as I frequently had in my early professional career. Whereas in first-class cricket my dismissal was rarely greeted with much celebration, back in club cricket whoops of happiness would greet my early demise. "This professional cricket is not all it's cracked up to be," I would hear muttered amongst the fielders.

It took me quite a while to get going and find my feet in a game that was for a while so unfamiliar.

Strangely enough MCC came to my rescue and invited me on several occasions to play at Lord's against MCC young cricketers and MCC schools. Inspired by playing on such a famous ground again and captaining MCC too against keen and talented young players, I felt more at home and began to behave more like a cricketer. I reverted to my normal routine and preparation, not quite back in the airing cupboard but along the same lines. Lord's somehow inspires players to great deeds, and I found that a fair amount rubbed off on me.

A great step forward in my rehabilitation came in 1992 when I was invited by MCC to lead a cricket tour to the Leeward Islands in the West Indies as player/manager. This came, I think, as a gift from heaven – four weeks of sea and sunshine amidst the world's most beautiful small islands. The purpose of the trip was to spread the cricketing word to some of the far away, less sophisticated parts of the Caribbean and persuade the locals that there was more to life than basketball and baseball whose popularity was gradually seeping in from America and diverting the locals away from their cricket.

In response to the Leewards invitation MCC selected a strong side. Nigel Briers as captain, Alan Fordham, Ian Hutchinson, David Ward, Stephen Henderson, Peter Moores, Graham Cowdrey, Bradley Donelan, Raj Maru, Nick Cook, Tony Pigott, Roland Le Febvre and Neil Williams.

In the event I only played in one match, in Nevis, a small volcanic island just a short boat journey away from St. Kitts. I appointed myself captain for the day. The ground, not far from the sea, looked very dry with a pitch so shiny and bare of grass that it could have been polished with beeswax. How would it play, I wondered? Had it been watered recently, and if so what would that mean? How much pace was to be expected? Would the bounce be even? Would it take spin? What sort of team did they have? What if we won the toss? It's no wonder that captains pace about with furrowed brows and a dry mouth prior to play starting.

As luck would have it, they won the toss and elected to bat. With this anxiety removed from my shoulders I felt more relaxed. And for a while all went well. The local team played hesitantly, and my bowling changes produced the desired effect and helped to peg back the run rate. That is, until the first drinks interval. While I was chatting to one of the umpires, a minor skirmish with the water trolley broke out amongst MCC's more playful characters, at the conclusion of which Bradley Donelan, in response to receiving a wetting, aimed a vigorous kick at Roland Le Febvre's backside at precisely the same time as Le Febvre swung his arm down by way of protection. The two limbs collided with a crunch and moments later Le Febvre made his way to the pavilion nursing a badly broken arm.

When play restarted, I was still unaware of the accident and stood at mid-off while Nick Cook bowled the next over. I received the news by way of 'Chinese whispers' which, starting with Peter Moores our wicketkeeper, worked their way around the covers to Graham Cowdrey who, halfway through the over, broke the news to me.

In all the matches I ever captained, both first-class and otherwise, never had one of my players been so severely injured at the hands of his own team. And I felt the lion's share of responsibility fell upon my shoulders as both captain for the match and manager.

The upshot of all this, although of no consolation to poor Le Febvre, was that we were a bowler short, Le Febvre being one of our important weapons as a medium pacer. As a last resort I threw the ball to Graham Cowdrey despite not being quite sure what he bowled. The Nevis batsman could not work out the mysteries of his slower ball (in fact none were very fast) and made a complete hash of things to such an extent that Cowdrey in 8 overs took six wickets for very few runs and turned the game in our favour – Nevis all out 134.

Mind you, this was no easy target against the fiery pace of Vaughan 'Hungry' Walsh and John 'the dentist' Maynard whose aggression had for some years been terrifying the local islanders. But on this occasion shrewd and brave batting from Hutchinson, Henderson, Cowdrey and Fordham saw us home to the target without further disaster.

Having played countless games of professional cricket in which the outcome was important, I found that my interest was once again stirred when Peter Lowndes persuaded me to captain the Eton Ramblers in the Cricketer Cup competition. This tournament involved 32 public school old boy teams in a straight knock-out with matches limited to 55 overs a side. It was both competitive and intriguing, ingredients that captured my attention. Among the schools were some fine players including a smattering of ex and current professionals. And all of a sudden I began to think again about batting orders, fielding positions, bowling line-ups and general strategy. Team availability was always a problem; from one match to another you could never be quite sure who you would see, commitment not being the strongest Rambler trait. It was all a bit hit and miss, but at least here was something to whet my appetite and get my teeth into.

At last, in my fourth year of trying we reached the final which was played at Vincent Square in central London and there we soundly beat Repton by 115 runs. Strangely enough for a Public School team, we had a fine bowling attack: pace, spin and swing, and not without control either. I felt I had found my niche, blending into the team unpretentiously and unburdened by the pressure of any longer playing a leading role. The transition from professional to amateur had been successfully concluded – and in 1993 I retired contentedly from the competition.

21

TWO TOURS TO THE EAST

England Under-19 tour to Sri Lanka, Dec 1993 – Jan 1994

In August 1993 I received a telephone call, inviting me to manage England's under-19 tour to Sri Lanka that winter. For some years I had been coaching England's age-group squads at Lilleshall Sports Centre in Shropshire under the supervision of Micky Stewart, who was then directing England's Development of Excellence programme. Yet, for all that, it was a surprise to be plucked from the relative obscurity of Arundel to manage some of the most promising young cricketers in the country.

Despite all the well-intentioned preparation in England, nothing could have prepared the youngsters for Sri Lanka's hostile climate, for which no fair-skinned European can be ready. That, coupled with the immense natural skill and flair of the young locals, made it a formidable challenge, but it was one from which the stronger players were able to learn and adapt.

Graham Saville from Essex was team coach and Dean Conway from Cardiff the physiotherapist. Three was enough, and we all played a full part. Graham, over many years, had developed an exceptional relationship with the young; he was both liked and respected. I was happy because I could bowl in the nets, sweating profusely, and help with fielding sessions. I got to know the players well and won their confidence. From that point onwards it was just a matter of serving them as best I could.

Despite many a gritty practice session and tactical team talk, the Sri Lankans were always a little ahead of our game. They won the three-match 'Test' series by one match to nil with one drawn (very much in Sri Lanka's favour) and one ruined by rain in Kandy. The one-day series of 50-over matches, we lost 2-1.

On dry pitches, surrounded by noisy fielders, we struggled to come to terms with the spinning ball. This was cricket being played in the market place and stemmed mainly from the exceptionally competitive nature of Sri Lankan school cricket. Their passion was compelling, their commitment irresistible.

Some of our players coped better than others, but the whole experience was a test of character as much as anything. The small management team had the task of trying to steer the young through some troubled waters and lift their spirits. I loved the challenge. It was right up my street.

Winning cricket matches is both pleasing and fulfilling. The fact that we spent most of our six weeks in the heat, with our backs firmly driven against the wall, took little away from the purpose of the tour. There was as much to be gained from defeat as there was from victory. Defeat tends to concentrate minds more acutely and demands more analysis and self-examination. One way or another we did a lot of losing in Sri Lanka, and from that the players stood a better chance of strengthening their resolve and technique for the future.

The hope and expectation was that one or two players would rise above the ordeal and progress to the next stage and onwards into Test cricket. On this tour we had two outstanding prospects: Michael Vaughan the captain, who opened the batting and bowled off-spinners, and Marcus Trescothick who, although a year younger than the others, had been promoted to a position where he could display his considerable potential.

Michael was the class player with the bat. He had presence at the crease and displayed an instinctive authority and determination not to allow the bowlers to dictate. Not easy. Leadership is no easy matter either at this level, with the patterns of the game less clear to young players. But Michael was a good listener, and his endearing manner helped him to understand the values of his team. A captain under pressure from the opposition will always learn more from the matches, and this was certainly the case with Vaughan in Sri Lanka.

While I have never considered myself a prophet, I did make a short entry in my tour diary on January 2nd 1994:

> *Michael shows all the signs of becoming a fine captain as well as being an outstanding player. In selection matters his judgement was calm, well-mannered and astute (and also in line with my way of thinking!).*

Composure is an important aspect of leadership.
Michael might be a great asset for England by 2002
and beyond.

Marcus Trescothick was at quite a different stage. Still well covered with what might be termed puppy fat, he was not fit enough to do himself justice in such a bubbling cauldron of activity. But he too showed signs of class as a batsman. He stood still and watched the ball – simple things – and he struck it as cleanly as anyone on the trip. I think he may have found Sri Lanka a tough environment to be thrown into – many do – the food, the smell and the heat not really to his liking. On most evenings he would slide off with his friends to the Pizza Hut adjacent to the hotel. It was tough for him. But he emerged from the ordeal a better and more confident player and person.

I took my managerial responsibilities seriously and, so far as I can remember, only slipped up badly once. Wet weather had ruined our visit to the beautiful city of Kandy in the middle of the island. With little play possible in this final 'Test' match we visited an elephant park and the Royal Botanical Gardens before exploring in the evening the mysterious Holy Temple of the Tooth, Buddha's most sacred shrine.

While it was good to wander about in Kandy, it was hardly compensation to the players for so little cricket and after four days, with the match abandoned, we decided to board our coach and make a bolt back to Colombo and to the one-day series.

It was a three-hour drive, and till about halfway I was enjoying it. Then I was suddenly gripped tightly by a horrible feeling. I remembered that back in the hotel in Kandy were all the players' wallets and passports, entrusted to me and safely locked up in the deposit box. Somehow I had to devise a plan for getting them back to Colombo, preferably without suspicion of incompetence falling upon me. My only hope lay in our devoted friend and baggage handler, Sirripala. On hearing the story, he insisted on returning to Kandy by bus.

That evening, back in the Taj Sumadra hotel, I was constantly pestered by players for both money and passports. It was a

Sunday evening, and I had to play for time by making out it was quite impossible to conduct transactions of any sort until Monday; wallets would not be helpful until then. Despite some wistful and disbelieving looks, I thought I had got away with it.

In the meantime I had dinner with Graham Saville, Dean Conway and Michael Vaughan and prayed fervently for Sirripala's early return. I was not disappointed. At 10 pm he crept up to our table in the dining room, looking exhausted, and told me that the mission was accomplished. At this point unfortunately my cover was blown and the truth had to be told, but I was so pleased to see Sirripala and the valuables that I did not really care.

It did not take long for the story to get out, and I was severely punished by the players at the next team meeting – on the dual grounds of inefficiency and duplicity.

The players had learnt a lot on the tour, and so had I.

England 'A' tour to India and Bangladesh, Jan & Feb 1995
Twelve months later I was off to India and Bangladesh with England's 'A' team.

For preparation we travelled to a remote hillside in Spain not far from Malaga where, against the odds, we found a cricket ground and practice nets, all surrounded by a herd of goats whose tuneful bells helped to add a special Spanish touch.

Spain was a good place to be in mid-December. It was warmer than England; the food, especially the fish, was good and it took our minds off Christmas and Christmas shopping. There was even time for some tourism – with a trip to the small hill town of Ronda, with its stunning views, followed by a visit to the bull ring, which was fortunately at rest.

Sound fitness and good health are prerequisites for a successful and happy tour. Alas, I lasted no longer than the fourth day of our Spanish preliminaries.

"Will you bowl at me in the nets?" Jason Gallian said to me after getting out in the practice match.

I confess that I was rather flattered to be asked, not having pitted my wits against a really good player for a fair while. Admittedly there were not many obvious alternatives from which he could choose. Nobody else was available, so it had to be me.

"Of course," I replied. "I'd love to. Good exercise."

So off we went to the nets to do what I am best at: giving batsmen confidence.

I was well into my spell and not doing badly when Jason asked me if I would mind bowling a few balls from around the wicket. This didn't bother me in the least. What I failed to remember was that I was running in and following through on an artificial pitch set on a stretch of concrete, elevated some two inches above the natural soil. Such was my enthusiasm – by now I was well into my rhythm and bowling with gusto – that I slipped off the edge of the matting and badly wrenched my ankle in the process. It was a disappointing end to a promising spell which had done much to raise Gallian's morale.

Help was close at hand in the shape of our physiotherapist, Wayne Morton, who came to my rescue with ice and strapping and some comforting words.

"What an idiot," he said, adding some rather more emphatic language. Wayne was a Yorkshireman.

From that injury onwards, Wayne became one of my greatest friends. An intelligent man, he combined a huge sense of fun with a professionalism which was scarcely ever matched by those around him. He loved cricket, though openly admitted to being far from fluent on the game's finer points. 'Inside-out over extra,' was a phrase which for a long time baffled him, as indeed it did many of us. He bowled endlessly and energetically in the nets and got everybody out at some stage. On all our tours together he was very good for morale – and, my goodness, there were times when he needed to be. Through thick and thin he became my closest ally and supporter.

India is a mysterious place and far from easy for us in the West to understand. The contrasts are so stark. The rich and affluent share the filth and noise with the poor and needy. Indecent greed and wealth stare out across the street at malnutrition and helplessness.

The harsh reality, with its frenzied and frantic scenes, hits you in the face without apology. Many cricketers swim happily along amidst the squalor and stay afloat, but some do not and join a sweaty dressing room of casualties caught out by the heat and stench and strange food.

Yet when I visited Chennai in 2002, managing England's blind cricketers for their World Cup, the squad responded to the whole experience as a great treat, greeting tummy trouble with a laugh, not a groan. Recovery was quick, and the cricket went well. Of course, this was more of a holiday with a purpose, a competition played by amateurs, but there was still an intense desire to succeed. We weren't the best team, but we reached the semi-finals where we lost to an efficient Pakistan side who went on to win the trophy. It was a pleasure to be with a team that was so much loved by both opponents and tournament organisers.

Chennai was still called Madras in 1994, and the England 'A' team arrived there in the second week of the tour. We had won a four-day match in Bombay, and spirits were high. Mark Ramprakash was our only casualty, struck down by a nasty bout of tonsillitis, but, before too long, this minor anxiety paled into insignificance as for the second winter running my guardianship of the team's valuables proved inadequate.

News arrived from the hotel that travellers' cheques, belonging to the team, had been found blowing about in the breeze all over the fourth-floor corridor. Exactly how poor Ramprakash was feeling I no longer really cared, for I felt sick myself.

I made haste, as far as that is possible in India, from the ground back to the hotel where I was able to see for myself the void in the safety deposit box where my £2,000 worth of cheques had once been stowed away. Where on earth had they gone? All afternoon, while the cricket proceeded calmly, I wretchedly tried to retrace my life over the previous twenty-four hours. But to no avail. I could only conclude that they had been stolen. An insider job, I calculated, as I eyed the entire hotel staff with suspicion. I was at a loss, distraught as I saw long shadows cast over my competence. This was far worse than the episode in Kandy.

That evening Keith Fletcher, England's head coach, rang from Australia. His tour was going from bad to worse, and he was bothered about injuries to his bowlers. We were both at a low ebb, so for some ten minutes we discussed fishing and fishing flies. Morale was lifted, and the trials and tribulations of life put back in perspective. The telephone call was money well spent.

I was sitting at the ground the next day, pondering my future, when a message was delivered to me from the hotel manager with the astonishing news that the cheques had been found with a lowly hotel worker who had apparently taken them from the deposit box. It was an unlikely story but, in the circumstances, I felt no desire to investigate further. I put the incident down to the paradoxical nature of things in India where honesty and dishonesty lead parallel lives, making it so hard to distinguish between the two.

From Madras, with a sigh of relief, we flew to Bangalore where we won our first 'Test' match against India 'A'. Ganguly and Dravid were the two up-and-coming Indian stars, but even they had their problems against Chapple and Cork.

From Bangalore we travelled to Delhi, which most English people look forward to visiting. The contrast between New Delhi and the Old City will strike to the heart of the least emotional being. On the one hand there is the majestic masterpiece of Edwin Lutyens' architecture, the Viceroy's residence, The India Gate and Government buildings all supremely British and notable for their elegance and perspective. Not far away is the sprawling mass of muddle, street markets and smell, which represents India of old. Amongst the shopping bazaars, of which there are many, there is great strength in the city, and within all the hustle and bustle stands the Red Fort which dates from the very peak of Mogul power and still remains a haven of peace.

Into this cauldron of chaos the England 'A' team found itself immersed in mid-January 1995. Prospects were good as we battled our way through the busy arrivals terminal in the evening with an early night seemingly within our grasp. We received the customary friendly welcome – garlands of flowers and red dot on the forehead – almost too friendly in fact and I could tell that something was wrong.

"Sadly," our Indian representative began to tell us, "there are no rooms available at the Taj Palace Hotel." He tried to soften the blow by explaining that, instead, rooms had been booked at the nearby Centour Airport Hotel. There was no immediate option available other than to board the bus and trundle off, somewhat disgruntled.

It was not a great spot, dark, dingy and stuffy, being blessed with neither windows nor effective air conditioning. As manager I resolved to set about the task of extracting us without saddening our hosts or causing too much trouble.

The following day I arranged for the team to take a trip to the Taj Mahal, waving them goodbye as they boarded the 5.30 a.m. train to Agra. Even at that time the platform was alive with people.

Now I could set about my mission. With Dominic Cork and Ian Salisbury, who had chosen not to make the trip, I made my way to the Taj Palace Hotel where I found they were busy refurbishing the fifth floor on which we had been supposed to stay.

"No, no, no, no, no," the manager said to me, frantically shaking his head. "You cannot possibly stay here."

Yet, despite the transparent clarity of the word 'no', his negative attitude gave me a chink of hope. It was merely an opening gambit prior to further negotiation and, with a modicum of persuasion, he was moved to see what could be done to make the rooms habitable.

All day long the fifth floor echoed to the sound of drills and saws and hammers and shouts of anguish, with Cork and Salisbury throwing their weight in behind the effort. The manager was something of a perfectionist so for a long time it looked as if we were getting nowhere. His high standards would have to be compromised – and eventually they were. The makeshift rooms had stone floors and plenty of sawdust, and very little paint, but by 8 p.m. our luggage was being moved into them.

Quite excited I was when I stood on the station platform, waiting for the 'Agra Flyer' to return at 10 p.m. and to spread the happy news that we were now safely, if a little uncomfortably, based at the Taj Palace. Morale was now high. The trip to the Taj Mahal had been much enjoyed, and the new surroundings were welcomed. It was a triumph for the extraordinary nature of the Indian spirit, its unpredictability reassuringly constant.

The cricket at Delhi, against the Indian Combined Universities, was not too demanding, and from there we travelled east to Calcutta where, despite the wide open spaces, millions are crammed together in shanty towns where disease and hunger share a putrid existence.

Yet my impression of Calcutta was of a place with smiling people. Taxi drivers were thrilled to discover that their passengers were both English and cricket lovers and, with the meter ticking away, a tour of the city was immediately on the cards.

The sight of cars, bicycles, lorries, rickshaws, street-traders and pedestrians all jostling for position on the Howrah Bridge made the M25 in the rush hour appear like a long lost friend. Little appeared to move on the bridge, the fumes were toxic, the river was filthy and yet life progressed at its own pace amongst cattle and scabby dogs. For most, this was a city of low expectations where a plate of food was a bonus. Yet I found I was never far away from a happy face in Calcutta where courage and humour abounded.

My first day there began with the exciting news that Mark Ramprakash had been called up to play in the full England team in Australia. As a result I had to pop into the main city early to arrange his travel plans and ensure him a comfortable passage to Adelaide – quite a challenge. As a player of the very highest class, Mark had deserved this opportunity more than most; I saw him off at the airport for his long and lonely journey via Bangkok and Brisbane.

I returned to the city in the late afternoon and set off to find the Missionary Orphanage in Circular Road where I hoped to meet Mother Theresa and her sisters of charity. When I arrived there, Mother, as she was generally known, was out. It was natural enough to feel a little disappointed, but my mood quickly changed when I was ushered into the building by two sisters, clad in their distinctive blue and white habits, and directed upstairs to the first floor.

I found myself in the company of about thirty young children, the eldest of whom might have been four at the most, and all sick or handicapped in some way. The atmosphere, though, was a happy one. The room was lit up by the smiles on the faces of the children who were sitting round wooden tables, eating their evening food – fish and rice. Most of the young, when they arrived at the orphanage off the streets, were desperately malnourished. Many did not survive and fell victim to common illnesses, but they were at least given a chance through the love bestowed on them by the sisters of charity.

After the meal came the ceremony of pots, possibly the most important event of the day's routine. Each infant was firmly placed, like it or not, upon his or her pot where they were expected to perform. Medicine was dished out as the nuns hoped to catch the children off their guard. But, with me looking on, there was little chance of much activity at either end. I was a distraction, there was not much doubt about that, and one which caused much amusement and funny faces.

We also visited a charity established by an Englishman and his wife who, after successful careers with the Hong Kong and Shanghai Bank, had turned their attention to the provision of sanctuary for Calcutta's lost and abandoned children. Connections in Hong Kong had inspired them to raise funds to establish a small school where children could grow up and receive an education. Many of the young were found starving, destitute and in despair at the two main railway stations in the city from whence a number were retrieved and given 'Future Hope', the name of the charity.

On tour there is rarely enough time to pursue activities that make a difference. But on this occasion, inspired by the enthusiasm of David Hemp, a cricket match was arranged between members of the England 'A' team and the 'Future Hope' school. The pitch was lively – rough and bumpy – but nobody cared much as the match got underway. Who won, I can't remember, and of course it didn't matter. In the hot sun there had been much running about and a lot of shouting and noise. It was, as it were, something of a replica of the street traffic outside.

The positive attitude adopted by the England players was reflected in their performances on the field. Between them they built up a ground-swell of confidence which became a godsend in the tougher moments. The second and third 'Test' matches were both concluded successfully after much uncertainty on the final days. David Hemp with a hard-hitting 99 not out steered England to a tricky target of 254 in Calcutta, and the tail enders – Patel, Johnson and Stemp – saw England home by one wicket on a turning pitch in Chandigarh. These were both courageous wins and, despite cutting things a bit fine, showed a resilience not always associated with the Englishman abroad.

Cricketers the world over will have you believe they are never given enough time off to recover from the exhausting life of professional sport. To a great extent this is true. They rattle around the world, playing a great variety of cricket in different places without much time to take stock. Match after match is played with no greater objective other than to justify the cricketers' existence in the world and fulfil the demands of the fixture card.

But at least in Bangladesh we had a little free time, and several of us decided that a game of golf would be a useful way of recharging the batteries. When we arrived at the clubhouse just outside Dacca, we were mobbed by an army of caddies all eager to do everything for us. And there were as many ball-boys too who, we found out later, would spread themselves out over the course ready to retrieve our balls or at least find them concealed in hideous 'lies'. After much hard and determined negotiation we ended up paying the full price for just about everything: hire of clubs, trolleys, balls, tees and all manner of bits and pieces.

Glen Chapple, Dominic Cork, Paul Nixon and Alan Wells played together because they were rather good. I played with Wayne Morton, David Hemp and Ian Salisbury, our combined fluency just about putting us into the duffer league. And indeed we did not play well.

My caddy looked at me in despair, raising his eyes to the clouds after a four-wood off the fairway skimmed flat across one of the many water hazards where, after briefly giving me hope by attempting a Barnes Wallis, the ball descended into the depths. At this point a young diver plunged in and retrieved it and then proceeded very persuasively to try to sell it back to me.

None of us played well. Hemp hit his ball into every pond on the course and lost his temper while Morton, a true Yorkshireman, never fully recovered from the cost of the round. The trade in balls continued all morning, and the mood reached rock bottom when Hemp's caddy ran back to him clasping his ball and claiming that a large bird had swooped down, picked it up and dropped it in the deep rough.

With our sense of humour long since gone, we were scarcely in the mood to be sold fish, recently caught in the water traps. Despite all this and in order to get away without too much trouble, I tipped the caddies generously. They are no fools, of course, and can spot a few Europeans from afar. Meanwhile the minds of the cricketers were briefly turned away from cricket.

After the final match in Bangladesh I collected from a local tailor two lightweight suits which had been made for me, one of which I had decided to wear to the party breakfast, Iftar, in the evening after the final match – to celebrate the end of Ramadan. Until 18.18 pm we sat in sombre mood with neither food nor drink, awaiting sunset and the siren that would echo over the city. It was not a particularly jolly way to start a party.

At the end of the supper I had to make a presentation of an elegant shield to the Bangladesh President of Cricket, who was also the foreign minister. But, to my astonishment and horror, when the President unwrapped his present, he stood there holding a white side-plate decorated with a blue S in the middle. It appeared that the wittier members of the team had substituted the shield for a piece of Sheraton Hotel crockery.

I was floundering a bit amidst the formality of the occasion and told a nonsense story about the plate being cast in the Potteries, hence the S for Stoke-on-Trent. The President, being a true diplomat, appeared perfectly happy to believe all I said, and it helped to put some life into the evening.

Later on, amidst much laughter, the correct item was delivered to the President who accepted it gracefully with words spoken in perfect English. "I knew it was all a bit of high-spirited tomfoolery."

The tour was over, and it had been a success.

22

ARRIVING IN SOUTH AFRICA

Both the Under-19 and 'A' Tours had gone well, and I had enjoyed them. Neither tour attracted much attention, and such attention as there was tended to look on the bright side or at the very least give us the benefit of the doubt. The development and preparation of England's most promising young players took place beyond the glare of publicity. Progress was private and much the better for it.

In early spring 1995 I settled back into the routine of Arundel cricket. The peace and tranquillity of my life remained unruffled until mid-July when I was surprised to receive an invitation from the Prime Minister, John Major, to attend a breakfast at Downing Street. It was a bright morning and, arriving a little early as one might for such an occasion, I sat on a bench in St James' Park and admired both the ducks and enthusiastic joggers showing off in London's sunshine. Fortified by the forces of nature, I felt prepared to tackle bacon and eggs, and the other guests, at Downing Street.

The purpose of this gathering was to give the Prime Minister the stage from which he could announce his new sporting strategy. He loved sport and believed that greater access to its opportunities would benefit the nation. He spoke with great passion, leaving us in no doubt that this was something very dear to his heart.

With the formal part of the occasion over, I was wandering about the garden clutching a croissant in one hand and a cup of coffee in the other when I was intercepted by Alan Smith, Chief Executive of the Test and County Cricket Board. After preliminary good mornings and a show of slight surprise at bumping into each other, Alan put on a serious face and said, "Johnny, we would like you to go to South Africa this winter and then on to the World Cup in India, Pakistan and Sri Lanka as Assistant Manager to Ray Illingworth." Raymond was now in charge of and responsible for the England team both as Chairman of Selectors and Tour Manager.

Without even pausing for a sip of coffee I said I would love to do the job, whatever it entailed. I was to look after the administration of the tour while Illingworth, with the assistance of John Edrich and Peter Lever, friends who had helped him to regain the Ashes in Australia in 1970, would take care of the cricket.

Throughout my county career I had always got on well with Illingworth, mainly in an admiring and distant sort of way. First with Leicestershire whom he steered to the County Championship in 1975 and then later back at Yorkshire, both as coach and player, he commanded respect. He was very much brought up in the old school as a tough Yorkshire professional. Silent and intimidating on the field, I found him a tougher adversary even than his team mate Brian Close — when he later captained Somerset.

I got to know him very well during the course of the tour. He would sometimes hold court over dinner, entertaining the players with a steady stream of stories, mostly about himself but funny nevertheless. Illy, as he is generally known, was rarely dull and knew the game as acutely as anyone I have ever known.

I was even pressed into service once or twice as his bridge partner to while away long evenings with nothing on television. The regulars were Mike Atherton, Malcolm Ashton our scorer and Philip Bell the team doctor. I just filled in from time to time and usually spoiled things for Illy who was disappointed by my inability to count effectively. He liked to win and throughout his life had been used to success. Even over the bridge table my performances were scrutinised with a furrowed brow, and blame for our failure as partners was routinely flicked across in my direction. Fortunately our partnership which formed the framework of the tour proved more effective.

The arrival of England's cricket team in South Africa in October 1995 was an important sporting event. It was the first time an official England tour party had visited South Africa since its isolation from world cricket. I doubt whether many could have anticipated the impact that Nelson Mandela's release from prison on Robben Island would have upon the nation – or the bravery with which President F.W. de Klerk began to dismantle the Nationalist government, paving the way for free and open elections in 1994.

The cricket tour was never far removed from the influence and inspiration of Mandela. He used his political antennae to good effect and, along with his advisors, rarely missed a trick. Indeed luck was on his side in those early days. Just a few months before our arrival, Francois Pienaar led South Africa to victory in the Rugby World Cup and Mandela was invited to join in the celebrations and wear the South African rugby jersey. With rugby still very much an Afrikaner stronghold, nothing could have been more symbolic than this gesture.

The early days on tour are often rather fun. It is a time of hope, before the losing sets in and spoils things. The tour of South Africa was no exception, and the entire community of Johannesburg made us feel very welcome. On our third day in the Republic and after a vigorous practice session at The Wanderers, we attended the Consul-General's party. This was a glittering occasion for more than 500 guests including representatives of the business community, members of the United Cricket Board of South Africa as well as a great many socialites, some of whom were particularly admired by the England team.

I was well aware in the past that players had not always been at their best in this sort of environment. But on this occasion they piled off the bus at the front gate of the Consul-General's residence and disappeared into the crowd. There was music and food and dancing to be getting on with. Much of the gaiety was inspired and led by the Consul-General's wife who, despite not being in the first flush of youth, took quite a shine to several of the young players who, I think, were slightly startled by the attention being given to them.

It was a great party. The occasional wild moments kept us all on our toes. Wayne Morton, our physiotherapist and not renowned for shyness on such occasions, and Mark Ilott, our fast left-arm bowler, joined the band on stage and, despite the drink having taken a slight hold, they just about did justice to

Bryan Adams – or it may have been Bruce Springsteen. The performance was well received by an audience who by then were prepared to applaud just about anything.

I became aware as my watch ticked on past one o'clock that I was going to struggle to fulfil my managerial duties that night. When we had left our hotel earlier in the evening, there were 18 people on board the bus. For our return journey I could only muster together three: myself, Mike Watkinson and Richard Illingworth (not to be confused with Ray) who by then was uncertain about where he was or which country he was visiting. It took the two of us, Watkinson and Barclay, to rescue Richard from the Consul-General's wife's clutches and bundle him into the bus outside. Most of the other players could not be found, and those that could certainly didn't want to return to the hotel.

The three of us survived the journey home all right, but it was never going to be easy to steer Richard from the bus, through the hotel lobby, into the lift (which unfortunately was one of those transparent affairs where the occupants were visible to all) and up to his room. Mike and I carried him in as discreetly as possible, but the girl on reception was more observant than we expected and spotted that all was not well.

"Oh dear," she said. "What's happened to him?"

Watkinson gave her a tired look and replied drily, "I think he's been hit by a truck" and left it at that.

Nikky Oppenheimer, who was our host for the first match of the tour, invited us all to play golf at the River Club, a beautiful course notable for smooth fairways and greens like carpet. The rough, although frequently unyielding, was not so much the worry as the amount of water, both running and still, spread about the course. There were large fish in the ponds, barbel I was told, and creatures like mini-crocodiles, which kept the adrenalin flowing.

I play golf infrequently. There is therefore only one shot that really concerns me: the first one. It is the only shot of the round that is likely to command any spectator interest, mainly from those awaiting their turn. I was nervous as I stood and watched the England players tee off.

Early in the queue was Ray Illingworth. There was a hushed and respectful silence as he addressed his ball. His backswing, moulded into shape by years of practice, was a strange one which included an eccentric wiggle at the top of the swing from which the club descended towards the ball. Raymond rushed his downswing a little, and the ball caught the heel of his club. Instead of travelling straight down the first fairway, it fizzed off to the left with some velocity in what, in cricketing terms, might be considered a mid-wicket direction or cow corner. The ball might have travelled quite a long way, had not one of the many ponds on the course cushioned the blow.

It was with much relief that I witnessed this unfortunate response to pressure. When the laughter had subsided, I was reminded how lucky golfers are, compared with cricketers, to have the chance to put things right after an early indiscretion.

It was a courteous touch, I thought, that beside the many water hazards were placed large nets which might well have been used to poach the sizeable fish but were in fact great sources of comfort to those wishing to retrieve their golf balls from the water. Illingworth did just that and had another go from behind the pond with more success this time.

England embarked upon its first-class programme with a four-day match in Soweto against a South African Invitation XI, led by Hansie Cronje, South Africa's captain. This was the first game of such significance to be played in the township which for decades had been synonymous with hardship, poverty and brutality, its population segregated from the white man by repressive laws.

We were breaking fresh ground, playing cricket on a relatively new and unsophisticated Oval. Police sirens wailed in front of and behind our coach as it drove into the South West Township (Soweto is a short form, not an African name).

184

History was being made; we were helping South Africa to embark upon a new era.

The ground was magnificently decorated with colourful marquees which would not have been out of place at Tunbridge Wells or Cheltenham. Stands for the crowds of spectators, and especially school children, had been erected and surrounded the playing area.

Three thousand children were bussed into the ground to watch their first ever game of proper cricket. What a treat there was in store for them. Not only did they see Atherton and Stewart batting fluently together but they also witnessed, just before lunch, the arrival of Nelson Mandela amidst a cavalcade of noisy cars and the beat of helicopter propellers. He was led round and introduced to all manner of people, including both teams and officials, and said time and again, "What a great honour it is to meet you." His humility and sincerity (the two do not always go together) have possibly been his greatest strengths since his release from prison.

After much handshaking and waving and chatting to as many school children as possible, the excitement gradually subsided and the cricket continued. Shortly after lunch Mandela slipped away back to Pretoria, a little more quietly than he had arrived, and things got back to normal. It had been like a royal visit but without as much protocol or organisation.

As the warm afternoon wore on, the English started to run out of steam. I, along with several others, began to detect the tell-tale signs of heavy eyes which signalled sleep. I turned to Devon Malcolm, who was sitting alongside and not due to bat for ages, if ever. I suggested that we take a walk around the ground. He welcomed the idea and, although we could persuade no one else to join us, we set off, clockwise, carefully progressing behind the stands where we were less likely to be observed. An ice cream would have been welcome so we made good speed to the furthest side of the ground from the pavilion where it was rough and bumpy.

We were just about to move on when the South African Youth Development Manager, Kaya Majola, saw us and suggested that we held an impromptu coaching class for some of the Soweto children watching the cricket. By now Atherton had been batting for a long time, in obdurate form, and it did not take much to persuade a large number of youngsters to leave the cricket and join in.

All of a sudden Devon and I had been put on the spot. There were a few bats, a handful of tennis balls and a smiling Devon Malcolm who seemed unphased by the challenge.

"What do you think?" I asked him, casting my eye upon a sea of expectant faces.

Devon's reply surprised me. "I think I shall teach them how to bat," he answered with a glint in his eye.

He took up the challenge with great gusto and, after a couple of demonstrations, the whole field was littered with children swishing about with bats and having the time of their lives.

This was certainly more fun than watching cricket. Half an hour later, exhausted by their exertions, the children sat down and listened to some wise words from our fast bowler before returning to their places in the stand.

When they had gone, we continued our walk and Kaya Majola came up to us again.

"Many thanks for that," he said. "I fear you might have just ruined a whole generation of South African cricketers."

23

PUT TO THE TEST IN SOUTH AFRICA

For much of my life I have rushed about in a great whirl of activity, feeling very busy but not always making much progress. There is a certain comfort in frantic activity. When in doubt, do something that looks important, even if it's only the manic use of a mobile telephone which has, for millions, become a comfort blanket.

For many of us it does not sit too well to look idle. In my small cricketing world I should say that in the last twenty-five years or so there has been a marked increase in frenzied rushing about, and I am not sure how much good it has done anyone.

It is not that I am opposed to exercise. In fact, I am very much in favour. I still go for a run, mainly on the machine at home, and feel better for it. But I am not so sure about the relentless programmes being asked of our professional cricketers day in, day out, throughout the summer. They arrive at cricket grounds shortly after breakfast and spend around two hours preparing for the long day's cricket ahead. And it is not gentle stuff. There is a lot of playing touch rugby and the like. Fielding drills, bowling practice, batting exercises and occasionally work in a net all form part of the rigmarole. In a way, this must enhance or top up fitness, perhaps help with the team ethic, but it is also sapping essential energy. The players do all this because they have to. Not to conform puts their position in jeopardy. Coaches feel duty-bound to supervise the programme. It is a part of their job; it is expected of them. To prepare effectively is all a matter of striking a happy medium between worthwhile activity and sensible relaxation. You will find normally that the worse a team is performing, the more frantic is its style of preparation. It should be the other way round.

In South Africa I became increasingly aware of the physical and mental demands made upon the cricketers. Exhaustion ran hand in hand with lack of form, for which the best possible remedy is often rest.

After a rain-affected draw in the first Test match in Pretoria, the second in Johannesburg was awaited with keen anticipation. From the moment England won the toss and were lured by a damp and slightly cracked pitch into electing to field, life became an intense struggle for the visiting team. South Africa made 332, England 200 and, hard though they tried, England could not make up the lost ground. The result was that just before lunch on the fourth day they were faced with an almighty task: to score 479 runs for victory or to bat for nearly two days to save the match.

From that point Atherton embarked upon one of the great rearguard actions of all time. His combination of physical and mental stamina, as well as a technique which withstood all of the devilry and skill of Donald and Pollock, gradually stifled and blunted the South African ambitions. He was grittily and bravely supported by Robin Smith and Jack Russell who both curbed all inhibitions in support of their captain.

The last day was made even more interesting for me by the activities off the field. Unknown to Russell, while he was batting so stoically, I was smuggling his wife Aileen through customs and into the Sandton Sun Hotel where we were staying.

Hitherto, Jack had never permitted Aileen to join him on tour for fear, I suppose, of distracting his considerable powers of concentration. Now here she was, a surprise, and certainly the last person on Jack's mind while the South African bowlers were peppering him with hostility.

With my delicate mission accomplished, I spent the afternoon in a state of agitation as the saving of the game became a possibility. Much of the time I sat quietly in the dressing room, half-watching the television with Dominic Cork who was for ages next man in. It was not an easy time for him. He went very pale, and I feared he might be sick at any moment. In the end he was not needed – but spare a thought for those whose part is never played.

The day ended in triumph. Atherton returned in glory, if not victorious, to the pavilion after his 643-minute innings. It was a study in batsmanship of the highest quality and, of its type, has been bettered by very few others in Test cricket. There was much celebration and jubilation, almost as if England had won the match – or even the series – neither of which was the case.

Later that evening both teams spent a noisy time at the Johannesburg Club, except of course for Russell who had completed one of the great matches of his career. He had broken the world record with 11 catches in the Test, then he had batted for well over four hours for an unbeaten and match-saving 29. And at the end of it all he discovered that, concealed in his room, was his wife. For him more than any other, it had been a day to remember.

Jack is an extraordinary chap, and he became one of my closest friends on tour. I instinctively warmed to his eccentric and deeply thoughtful character, which was so out of the ordinary. From an early stage in his career Jack had dedicated himself to the pursuit of excellence both as a wicket-keeper and batsman. Alan Knott, perhaps the most accomplished of all all-rounder wicket-keepers, was his mentor and coach. They came from the same stable.

On tour, Jack would shut himself away for long periods at a time and emerge only to fulfil his cricketing duties and keep himself fit. His diet was a strange one. He had little faith in any unfamiliar and foreign food and stuck religiously to a regime of Heinz Baked Beans washed down with many cups of tea. He would bring most of his supplies with him from England and lived in fear of running out.

His cricket equipment, and especially his wicket-keeping gloves, were equally important to him. He would forever be sewing his gloves or his inners together, patching up his pads and batting gloves or adding extra bits to his helmet. Jack was a master with the needle and thread, which he made use of even when they were not needed.

An accomplished artist too, he brought his easel on tour along with paper, canvasses and painting equipment, and he was never happier than when he was sitting on his stool in front of an African scene, paints at the ready. The Zulu War was one of his favourite subjects. He never went far without Stanley Baker and Michael Caine and their famous film close by his side, and he drew inspiration for his paintings from Rorke's Drift and the surrounding Natal landscape.

But the most treasured item of all Jack's possessions, and one which I presume would be his luxury on a desert island, was his white floppy hat. This hat, which he had acquired early in his career, was central to his life as a cricketer. Without it, he felt naked and uncertain, indeed he used its rim so that he could line up the ball from the bowler's hand. I cannot say that it was a particularly attractive piece of clothing, a little grubby and inevitably frayed at the edges and patched up in parts with material from Jack's collection. Like a teddy bear in years gone by, Jack's hat was his best friend and he did not play cricket without it.

The hat was not a trouble-maker by nature but, when Ali Bacher of the United Cricket Board for South Africa suggested that Jack should not wear his hat in the one-day internationals, I was forced to remonstrate and take Bacher to task on this issue. The difficulty was caused by coloured clothing and the sponsors' requirement for England to play in pale blue, hats included. There was quite a furore which involved messages passing backwards and forwards from South Africa to England.

In the future I could see that sponsors and television were going to meddle in everything, probably dictating the course of international cricket, but for now I was on Jack's side: fighting for both freedom and flexibility!

In the end, after careful negotiation, a compromise was reached. In the first few matches Jack wore his hat. After that, using his dexterity in the sewing department, he skilfully stitched a pale blue hat onto his own treasured white one. Jack was happy with the outcome and so were Bacher, the sponsors and indeed the match referee, Cammie Smith.

For a while at least, Jack's hat had delayed the advance of the dangerous and ever more powerful currents of commercialism.

It was a weary party that clambered on board a flight to Paarl in the Western Cape the morning after the draw at Johannesburg. What everyone needed was a rest before the third Test match in Durban. I decided that Atherton, more than anyone else, after his marathon innings, needed a break.

The team had been booked into an old-fashioned Dutch guest house, called the Zomerlust Hotel. It was a beautifully designed building draped with vines and wild plants. The rooms were spacious and all different from each other with large vases of flowers to welcome us. You might think that an international cricket team would not notice such things, but there you would be wrong. With a backdrop of mountains and vineyards all around us, the England players had the run of the place – no other guests – and could not possibly have been more contented.

Surely, I thought, this was what a tour was supposed to be like and, I imagine, would have been in years gone by. This was far removed from the busy international hotels of the big cities, all hustle and bustle and filled with the grimness of modern living – lap-tops and mobile phones at every turn. Here we could relax. There were simple pleasures – a drink, a cup of tea and a swimming pool – just what a tired man would wish for.

Amidst this tranquil environment there was still some cricket to be played, a rather more friendly game against Boland. Some of the more exhausted players were excused this match. Mike Atherton was one of these, and to my surprise, expressed an interest in fishing, not a sport he had ever tried. So, with my great friend Andrew Wingfield-Digby, a day's outing on the Berg River was arranged with the help of our enthusiastic guide, Peter Longmore.

He took us to a lively stream up in the hills where the water bubbled and bounced from rock to rock and pool to pool. Peter assured us that there were fish to be caught but, beautiful though the river was, it was not easy for a beginner or even an experienced fisherman for that matter. Dressed in hat, shorts, t-shirt and trainers, it did not take Atherton long to get the gist of casting a fly and, once he had got going, he made it clear that he didn't want any spectators.

We pushed off upstream and left him to it. Every now and then I did look round to see how he was getting on. His wading was uncertain. My main memory is one of the England captain frequently disappearing up to his neck in water as he trod unsteadily through the pools.

It quickly became clear that Atherton's temperament was as well-suited to this new-found sport as indeed it was to cricket. It seemed that he was happy to cast a fly for hours onto a pool with only the very slenderest hope of success, not entirely dissimilar from his batting where his patience had become legendary. When it comes to fishing and cricket, there is no greater virtue.

He did not catch a fish on this occasion, his debut with the fly – indeed he had failed to trouble the scorers when he began his England career against Australia at Trent Bridge in 1989 – but he caught the fishing bug and has since fished all over the world with much success.

We returned that evening to Zomerlust with four very respectable trout which Andrew and I had lured from the rough water. These were cooked for us by the proprietor herself, a round and jolly lady of rosy-cheeked countenance, and fed not only us fisherman but several of the players too. With our faces glowing as the night wore on, we all concluded that, by way of relaxation and recuperation, our day in the mountains and by the riverbank could hardly have been better spent.

The early part of this historic tour was plagued by rain, and rain continued to torment us when we travelled up the eastern coast of South Africa to Durban which was hot, humid and very wet. It did not put off the surfers, though, who relentlessly tackled the steeply curving waves of the Indian Ocean. Fishermen too were successful from the pier which jutted out into the grey sea. They caught silver fish called shad (or something like that), not unlike a salmon, which they laid out on the concrete in the rain.

Persistent storms set in and ruined the Test match when honours were just about even after two days. It had been overcast, hot and oppressive, and I suppose it came as little surprise when this much-awaited match had to be abandoned just as the first Test at Pretoria had been a month earlier. It was very disappointing for everyone, especially the hundreds of supporters who had travelled all the way from England for the occasion.

In the absence of much cricket in Durban, the most exciting and challenging episode so far was the arrival of a great party of players' wives, girlfriends, children, nannies, parents, even grand-parents, to join us in the gloomy weather.

From Assistant Tour Manager, overnight I was transformed into an untrained Thomas Cook representative. It was a responsibility I had not really bargained for, and I got off to a bad start. Having safely gathered in the new and excited arrivals, including my own family, Mary-Lou, Georgie and Theo, it was drawn to my attention that we were one short. By a process of elimination which took some time, it seemed that John Crawley's girlfriend, Kate Ward, had gone missing and, for all the searching of the airport, could not be found.

I think it may have been Mike Atherton's girlfriend, Isabel Careiras, who first gave me a clue to her whereabouts. She had noticed that Kate had taken a seat to the rear of the aircraft reserved, in those days, for smokers; at Johannesburg, perhaps she had failed to transfer with the others to the Durban flight, flying on to Cape Town instead. And indeed that is what had happened. It was quite a relief to tell Crawley of her mistake; he did not seem in the least bit surprised.

A century previously large armies were successfully moved on horse and foot over the vast plains and hilly landscape of South Africa. Yet, despite the help and comfort of modern communications, I found it quite a challenge to move a tour party of something nearing a hundred from Durban to Port Elizabeth in the Eastern Cape and then onwards to Cape Town.

It was fun having the families there. It changed the chemistry of the tour, and a rather more holiday atmosphere replaced the hard-nosed approach of the earlier days. So erratic over the years have England's performances been that it was hard to judge what effect, if any, they actually had. Leaving aside the cricket, the presence of this team of supporters, for that is what they were, added a little sparkle to the sometimes grim and entrenched nature of cricketers abroad. They lightened up the atmosphere.

In Port Elizabeth for the fourth Test match there was a big crowd and, for once, fine weather. For the most part South Africa were on top, but on the fourth day we did take a flurry of wickets which just might have tipped the balance.

Two things made the match memorable for me. The first was the African band and singers who staged a concert throughout the match which was powerful and tugged at the emotions. The second was the bowling of Paul Adams, playing in his first Test match aged 18. From his background, in the same Cape Town township where Basil D'Oliveira was brought up, he had developed a bowling action of such extreme unorthodoxy that it baffled many batsmen. As a left-armer, he disconcertingly looked behind him as he released the ball and it spun, quite sharply, mostly away from right-handers. But to confuse matters he also spun the occasional ball in.

The match, although drawn, had its moments. Neither team in such a close and emotive series was going to give an inch.

The road show moved on to the New Year finale in Cape Town where in the end England were worn down and worn out by a good South African side, well led by Hansie Cronje and enhanced by the eccentric skills of Paul Adams. 'After clinging tenaciously to equality throughout the series, England finally fell off the precipice at Newlands,' wrote Matthew Engel, the editor of *Wisden.*

It was not quite as simple as that. We had arrived in Cape Town full of hope. After all, we had batted well at Centurion Park before the heavens opened; saved the game so spectacularly at the Wanderers that we almost felt we had won it; a stalemate in the humidity and wet of Durban, and honours were just about even in Port Elizabeth.

The swift decline and fall from grace in Cape Town came as something of a shock. It was not an event that even Illingworth could easily take in his stride. On an uneven pitch, where variable bounce prevailed, the batsman of both teams were put to the test. Only Smith for England and Cullinan for South Africa offered much resistance and by mid-afternoon on the second day South Africa, in reply to England's meagre score of 153, were themselves poised perilously on 171 for nine.

There then followed the truly pivotal episode of the series when Paul Adams, who up until then had only faced 16 balls in first-class cricket, joined the more experienced Dave Richardson to see if they could extend the lead a little. This they did by adding 73 runs for the last wicket and, in doing so, drained both energy and morale from the England team. It was an episode which every proud English cricket player and supporter would wish to forget but, with thousands of English tourists crammed into the ground beneath the hot sun, it was never going to be an occasion that would pass without comment.

South African momentum was initially helped on its way by a wild English throw which went for four overthrows, followed by eight leg-byes and a 'chinese' cut from Adams which added four more to the score. Discouraged by all this misfortune poor Devon Malcolm, in his determination to polish off the tail-ender, bowled such a wayward spell that not even Adams was much troubled. The game quickly slipped away from England.

Cracks that had already begun to appear earlier in the tour, and had perhaps widened a little as recently as Port Elizabeth, now burst wide open. Illingworth, who had watched all this from the stand, could bear it no longer and, when the South African innings finally ended, he could not contain himself. He vented his frustration and wrath upon Malcolm. While Atherton and Stewart were fumbling with padding and velcrose, the tantrum continued until the storm finally blew over and England began its second innings.

Lest the point be missed, it must never be forgotten that Illingworth only behaved as he did because he really cared. After all he was Chairman of Selectors, Manager of the Tour, Head Coach and our first contact with the media. By 1995 this was almost certainly a bit much and needed to be diluted somewhat.

The outcome, row and all, was that we lost the Test series, deservedly so, at the last gasp. We lost because South Africa were a stronger side, not by a long way but just enough to make the difference.

Ultimately English morale had been shattered, and we lost the series of one-day internationals 6-1. It was a triumph for the new South Africa, matching the Rugby World Cup success the previous June. With Mandela at the helm, they were firmly on the sporting map as well as the international stage.

24

THE WORLD CUP

The World Cup in 1996, a tournament which followed directly on the heels of England's exhausting South African tour, was scheduled to be played in India, Pakistan and Sri Lanka although, sadly, a couple of bombs in Colombo put paid to the last part of that plan.

There was scarcely time to regroup after South Africa and certainly no time to think about cricket. That, of course, may have been a good thing. An overnight flight plunged us from the heat of Africa to the damp and cold of England in February, and hardly had we adjusted than ten days later we were flying off to Lahore to begin a new and entirely different campaign. The wounds had hardly had enough time to heal.

I love the sub-continent with a passion which explains why I have visited it so often and always looked forward to returning. For many of my cricketing friends it has had the opposite effect, causing them to think longingly of a pint of warm beer and James Alexander-Gordon reading the football results. Without a love of the people and culture, the chances of success on the cricket fields of India and Pakistan are very slim. It has not been a trait which English cricketers have mastered well and so, over many years, success has been scarce.

England began its preparation in Pakistan, Lahore in fact, not far from the Indian border and Amritsar where the Golden Temple, holy shrine of the Sikhs, adorns the city. We made our headquarters at Aitcheson College, Pakistan's most exclusive school where Imran Khan received his education. We practised hard in Lahore and even played a couple of matches against local opposition.

We seemed to be getting into the swing of things, and in my diary I wrote, 'Amazingly the matches went to plan.' Nobody was yet ill so we were at least in fair fettle to undertake the long journey to Calcutta for the World Cup opening ceremony.

In recent years opening ceremonies have become the in-thing, bigger, brasher and infinitely more lavish than the occasions merit. The event at Eden Gardens, Calcutta, in front of 130,000 paying spectators, was just about as stunningly awful as anything could be.

The dancing girls had not received their special dresses in time; the compere, disadvantaged by the darkness, mixed up the different countries and the players. Then came the laser show; not knowing what it was supposed to be like, I sat back and enjoyed it. Later, however, when I congratulated the Frenchman responsible for it, I realised from his steely, narrow eyes and the curl of his mouth that it had not, in fact, gone to plan. So angry were the Indians that there were calls for Jagmohan Dalmiya, the World Cup convenor, to be arrested and charged with wasting public money. Looking at the overall state of Calcutta and its starving population, it would have been a hard charge to deny.

At four o'clock the next morning, showing remarkable teamwork, we caught a flight to Ahmedabad in Gujurat. There we played New Zealand in our opening match and lost narrowly before pushing on to Peshawar on Pakistan's north-west frontier. Here we were perilously close to the border with Afghanistan and, with tribal feuds so prevalent, there was sadly no possible opportunity to venture the twenty miles or so up to the Khyber Pass.

Overlooked by snow-covered mountains in the distance, the cricket and cricket ground seemed something of an afterthought in this sombre backwater. We did at least manage to beat the United Arab Emirates quite easily, but this was not without casualties. Poor Craig White in his second over pulled his side muscles so badly that an immediate replacement was necessary and then, later in the day, Neil Smith was violently and rather publicly sick while batting.

The upshot of all this was that Dermot Reeve joined the squad, and White went home before the initial skirmishing was over.

Several of the players, including Graeme Hick and Reeve, felt short of practice. Because of this I taxied over to the main stadium to see whether any nets could be arranged. I was making limited headway, struggling to make myself understood by the ground staff who were, not surprisingly, unaccustomed to the English language, when I made a tactical error. I suggested that I would be perfectly happy to pay for any extra work they would have to put in. This idea was accepted with a smile, and about a dozen English cricketers subsequently made use of one rather shabby net in the corner of the ground. It was better than nothing, just, and the staff were duly paid.

The next day, when we were due to have a full practice session, a row broke out. My groundsman friend had spoken to a local journalist and had accused me of offering him a bribe in return for net facilities. It did go to show just how careful one has to be.

Despite this small drama we did manage to beat Holland a little unconvincingly but without further disaster. We moved on from Peshawar to Rawalpindi by bus, crossing the vast River Indus valley for our next match with South Africa, who after our recent experiences in their country rather had the edge over us.

It had been wet in Rawalpindi, and this had dampened the outfield and slowed down the pitch. All this might have been turned to our advantage, but in fact South Africa trounced us with a display of bowling and fielding that could scarcely have been bettered. It was a muddly day, too. No lunch at lunchtime, which is always a disappointment, four arrests outside the ground and a fire in one of the stands.

The press conference after the match was lively and Atherton, despite making nought, was surprisingly full of beans. We had been herded into a little room, and the atmosphere was highly charged. Ray Illingworth was not in attendance. All was going well initially until, out of the blue, a chap from a local Rawalpindi newspaper kept annoying the other journalists by constant and uncalled-for interruption. It was a wonder that nobody hit him. Eventually, Atherton, in exasperation, asked under his breath whether this tiresome buffoon could be removed. His remark was not picked up by the assembled journalists at the time, and it was only later that the word buffoon was identified on one of the more sensitive recording devices commonly used by the press. The Pakistanis in Rawalpindi, never slow to take umbrage, complained of a wicked slur upon their nation, made slightly worse by the inference of one or two who thought Atherton had used the word 'baboon' and not 'buffoon'. In the end an apology from Atherton seemed to do the trick and satisfy hurt feelings. The show continued but with the promise of success becoming ever more distant.

The arrival of Dermot Reeve had caused me some far from restful nights. He landed in Peshawar and, although not immediately selected in the side, was at once required as a 12th man to field occasionally and act as a drinks waiter – all part of the routine.

At first he could not be issued with his shirts suitably named on the back so I lent him mine. The upshot of this was that, from the moment Reeve arrived in Pakistan, I was pestered on the telephone by an assortment of girls asking me out at all hours of the night. Trying to explain to girls who could not speak English that I was not the required target became very tiring and tiresome. As I have said, touring in India and Pakistan is filled with improbable and puzzling events but is never dull.

England did not last much longer in the tournament, being overwhelmed by Sri Lanka's flair when, at Faisalabad in the quarter final, they showed us a fresh style of cricket. England had been left behind by players whose last thought in life was defence. Jayasuriya, Gurusinha, de Silva and the captain Ranatunga thrilled the crowd with their audacity and bombarded them in turn with their big hitting. They were to prove so effective that, with aggression to the fore, Sri Lanka went on to win the World Cup for the first time in its history.

25

ATHERTON'S FIRST CATCH

I rounded a corner of the River Deveron in Aberdeenshire and was confronted by the unlikely sight of four fishermen peering from the top of an old wooden bridge, as if playing Pooh sticks, into the pool below. I had just completed an unsuccessful morning flogging the water myself and was now interested to see whether the young enthusiast, Mike Atherton, was having better luck.

From casting his first fly in South Africa on a bubbling mountain stream between Paarl and Worcester, he was hooked and now could almost be described as a fanatic. Equipment, books, *Trout and Salmon* subscription, fly-tying kit, fishing lessons: it had all become pretty serious. 'Patience, Perseverance and Persistence' had become his watchwords. Exciting isn't it?

I could hear quiet mutterings on the bridge – tactics I presumed – and I spotted the occasional knowing stare into the water. Atherton's rod and line were being prepared for action and bait of some sort (not to be disclosed) fastened onto the hook. The three fishermen then dispersed to either side of the river, leaving Atherton on the bridge alone.

He prepared himself for that crucial first cast – vital to get it right first go, just like bowling that first looping, dipping, devious leg-spinner to some unsuspecting new batsman. The fish, a salmon, was unlikely to be fooled by a splashy muddle landing on his head – the equivalent of a long-hop or full toss. No, it must be perfect. Whoever said fishing was a peaceful and relaxing sport?

I stood motionless as Atherton prepared to cast; the crowd would have been silent, had there been one. Into the water went the bait with a plop, and I watched the line slowly come over the fish. A little twitch – no, my imagination. Yes, a tightening, a boil, a splash, a shout, and he was on. The captain of England was never prone to panic, but the hooking of his first salmon had him side-stepping this way and that on the bridge.

"Get off the bridge" shouted his three ghillies from the bank, and this was quickly followed by a series of barked instructions. "Keep your rod up ... keep the line taut ... let him run ... wind in ... don't hold him too hard." Fortunately, Atherton took no notice but muttered a selection of vocabulary normally reserved for tiresome cricketing opponents.

By now the fish was tiring and gradually, amidst much agonising, drawn to the net and landed. "That's one for the pot," Atherton said.

But before he could go on, the owner of the fishing suggested that the great fish, just about a seven-pounder on a good day, should be returned to the water. And so, reluctantly, the salmon was eased back to resume its quest for spawning grounds upstream. With a combination of pride and sadness Atherton, with a baleful look, watched his fish swim away to freedom.

I walked on down to the bridge. "Any luck?" I asked cheerfully as I got near.

"Yes, I've just caught my first salmon."

There can surely be few better moments in life to share than this.

26

ZIMBABWE

Within twelve months of visiting Mandela's South Africa, the England cricket team made a visit to Zimbabwe. The contrast in style and emotion could not have been more stark. Whereas South Africa was embarking upon a new journey stimulated by the potential of freedom, Zimbabwe was gripped by the rule of fear and intimidation.

Illingworth was no longer the tour manager and head coach. He had selected the tour party after which he honourably stood down from his position as Chairman of Selectors. In his place David Lloyd was appointed head coach, with John Emburey as his deputy. I was now the manager, my chief responsibility being for the organisation and administration of the tour.

Early on, we attended a reception at the British High Commissioner's residence in Harare, one of the few formal functions that were laid on. The High Commissioner suggested to me that we should dispense with the speeches. Yet, with the benefit of hindsight, I wonder if the tour would have gone better if I had insisted on speaking that evening. It was something I could have done well, and it might have helped to create a more positive relationship between us and our hosts.

As it was, the tour quickly went downhill. Our performances on the field declined from bad to worse, and it did not take long for things to get out of hand. A rampant band of press men descended upon Harare, and they made sure their readers back at home had something to get their teeth into. It was my first full England tour as manager, and it was a very different experience from the Under-19 and 'A' tours I had run.

From the start the international airport near Harare gave us an unfriendly introduction. The customs officials were both hostile and unhelpful, angering the travelling photographers by confiscating much of their equipment. It was evident at this early stage that no amount of charm or diplomacy would have much effect upon those having to operate under Mugabe's despotic regime. Only through tireless persuasion and negotiation were the cameras released.

This had been an ill-conceived and poorly planned tour. Zimbabwe had only recently been elevated to full Test match status, and it was hardly a secret in the cricketing world that England had voted against this promotion. Nonetheless this inaugural tour of Zimbabwe was considered a necessity and crammed in around Christmas and New Year, prior to a longer tour of New Zealand. It was a graceless exercise, arranged more out of duty than anything else, by the dying embers of the Test and County Cricket Board before the newly formed England and Wales Cricket Board had taken a hold.

Good and careful preparation is the key to success. It is easy to underestimate the effects of travelling overseas. In years gone by, when everyone travelled by boat, training and strategy could be discussed while players slowly got used to the change of climate. Now we all rush around the world in the same carefree manner that one might catch a bus to Brighton. No longer are there proper tours with a good spread of cricket and with a chance to see the country and get a feel for the people. Now it is more a case of dropping in for a Test match or two. It saves money and keeps the families at home happier. But it does not really work.

How easy it is to forget that Johannesburg, Pretoria and Harare are perched 6,000 feet up on the high veldt. That takes a bit of getting used to. So does Australia, especially Brisbane which is semi-tropical and where Australia usually schedules its first Test match. They are not stupid down under. India and Pakistan take a lot of getting used to as well, and Sri Lanka is just about the hottest place in the world. You cannot prepare for these places at home in England; you have to get out there and immerse yourself in their culture and cricket. Only then have you got half a chance. My guess is that we have rather forgotten about acclimatisation in the planning process.

In Zimbabwe we were woefully unprepared to compete with an emerging and talented cricketing nation and against players who, despite a charming exterior, were as tough as they come. There was an amateur spirit that ran through their cricket. They played for enjoyment and pride. Cricket for them must have been a welcome escape from the ghastly life to which they were being subjected.

Good preparation is a mental process; there needs to be a passionate desire to succeed. Our determination in this department was sadly lacking and for some reason, especially during the early stages of the trip, it seemed to me that the squad was suffering from an epidemic of mild depression. This may, in part, have emanated from Mike Atherton and the chronic injury to his back as well as a mixture of ailments to other members of the team.

The main problem, which I only fully understood once the tour was well under way, revolved around David Lloyd, our coach. For all their good nature and courtesy, the Zimbabweans could not bring themselves to like him. In fact, they could not stand him. Apparently the problem had begun some nine months earlier when David travelled to Zimbabwe with England's Under-19 team. Clearly all parties had rubbed each other up the wrong way, and there did not now appear to be any way of arranging a truce. It was both vexing and inconvenient and explained, to some extent, why local arrangements and practice facilities were so poorly organised. It became quite clear that few people, least of all members of the Zimbabwe Cricket Union, were going to lift a finger to help Lloyd.

As a result, strange things happened. We attended a scheduled practice session at the Harare Sports Club about a week into the tour. It was as if nobody had expected us to be there at all. There was no key to the dressing room, no nets, no stumps, no drink and little interest taken. The locals did not like Lloyd and in turn did not like England; not much was going to change that.

I did not blame them really. Life in Zimbabwe was pretty grim, and the presence of the England team was hardly improving things. We had become a grisly bunch, not made better by some inept performances on the field. It was a great relief to escape from the hot and claustrophobic atmosphere of Harare and to fly to Bulawayo and make a fresh start.

The wide streets of Bulawayo gave us a bit of breathing

space. No sooner had I reached our hotel than I found a message from the Zimbabwean team manager, Dennis Streak, father of Heath who would be leading the opposition bowling attack. He invited any number of us to visit his farm about two hours' drive away. We took up the offer with gusto, and quite a party of us set off into the wilderness led by Andrew and Guy Whittall in their sparsely sprung trucks. It was a bumpy journey, and bones were rattled and rumps sore by the time we reached the Streaks' farm.

The rainy season had turned pastures around the farm very green with the grass long, lush and growing furiously. The Streaks had planned a wonderful day. There was food and drink, plenty of it, at their 'camp' in the bush, and stone buildings which provided luxury accommodation. This was a whole world away from our cricket and a great escape from a campaign which was hardly bringing out the best in us.

Fortified by a wholesome lunch and much good-natured banter, we embarked upon an afternoon of hunting which involved attempting to shoot game in the bush. In fact, with only birds available as prey, it was an opportunity to see zebra, giraffe, buck, warthog and wildebeest. As the hunting party, armed with rifles, left the farm with hopes and enthusiasm high, it began to pour with rain.

I chose an altogether more gentle option and, with John Emburey and Nick Knight, sauntered down to the nearby lake and fished for catfish. Here we were successful and, with rain water running down our necks, we caught a great many of those ugly whiskery specimens, quite inedible, and returned them to the pond which was their home. Later we made our way back to the farm for tea, completely drenched but proud of our efforts. The shooting party was also in a bedraggled state, made worse by experiencing a disappointing afternoon in the bush. The pouring rain had caused the animals to lie low, and the birds remained unharmed. It is expectation that can so often be the devil. Expect nothing, and you will rarely be disappointed.

Despite the rain and lack of success in the bush, it had been one of our best days on tour and spent with courageous people who, for our sakes, turned their back on the acute sadness of their crumbling country to give us a day of unimpaired pleasure.

Returning from the Streaks' farm, we felt refreshed, refuelled and better equipped to tackle the first Test match which was fast creeping up on us in Bulawayo. Five-day cricket is still superior to any other form of the game, a complete test of skill and stamina where body and mind join forces to produce the ultimate performance. To this day cricketers still apply themselves to this marathon journey as a first priority above all else.

Before every Test match, there is much huffing and puffing. Practice is obligatory, conducted as much to keep the press and photographers happy as anything else; preparation tends to be something of a sham, a ritual to be endured rather than time spent honing skills for the battle ahead. For all that, it does give everyone the chance to feel at home on a new ground, to be comfortable with the dressing-room arrangements and, above all, the loos which are central to the routine of every cricketer and a very important part of the scheme of things.

The ground authorities were putting the finishing touches to the occasion which added to the Christmas holiday atmosphere while the match referee and umpires strolled about casting a critical eye upon the proceedings. The referee for this game was the Indian batsman from the 1960s, Hanumant Singh. Although a charming man and one with whom I struck up a firm and important friendship, his style differed markedly from that of his colleagues Clive Lloyd and Tiger Pataudi, neither of whom could ever have been accused of taking themselves too seriously. Possibly this was because, in their day, they had been great players in their own right and had little to prove other than to confirm themselves as good people with a sense of humour.

Hanumant Singh, by comparison, bustled about his duties as a keen traffic warden or policeman might. After paying close attention to the contents of our dressing room, I asked him whether everything was satisfactory.

"You are all fine," he replied, or at least that is what I thought he said.

"That's great," I said.

"No, you are all fine," he persisted a little more vehemently.

"Terrific," I said and set off to watch the players practising.

"No, no, you do not understand," he said, beginning to raise his voice a little. "You are all fined".

"Oh dear," I spluttered. "That's bad. What for?"

He looked at me severely. "It's the logos on the bats. I have measured them and they are too large, so you are all fined."

Nothing ever happened, of course; nobody was much interested in the size of the logos.

The nature of cricket is such that, for long periods, the game meanders along, quietly going nowhere. Then, suddenly, it springs to life and all hell lets loose. This was the pattern of the first Test match in Bulawayo, the final afternoon in rich contrast to the first four and a half days' play. All of a sudden England, whose performances so far on tour had been lack-lustre in the extreme, were in a position to win the match. It had been hard-going on a good batting pitch to take wickets, but Tufnell had come into his own with a fine spell of enlightened bowling. England, as a result, needed 205 runs to win the match from a possible 37 overs on the final afternoon: not out of the question.

It was a scorching hot day, and England lost Atherton early. But from then on Nick Knight and Alec Stewart began to play fluently and with increasing confidence. Amidst hysterical scenes in the crowd and with emotions running high, the target was steadily whittled down and came into view.

By the end both teams were fighting for their lives. The bowlers tried to slow the scoring down by bowling wide and stretching the goodwill of the umpires to the utmost. But remember, this was a Test match, not a one-day international. Tempers were a little frayed by now and Hanumant Singh for a while really did have his work cut out – with things that mattered. After all the fuss and excitement, when the last ball had been bowled, the scores were level and this for the first time in Test history. The match was drawn. This inaugural Test between the two countries had not been a disappointment.

The deeply passionate and competitive nature of the game quickly subsided as celebration took the place of combat. Drinks were shared by the players in the dressing rooms and Nick Knight, the hero of the day, was gradually brought back to the world of the living after his exertions in the heat of battle.

Meanwhile I plodded off with Mike Atherton to the post-match press conference held in the clubhouse dining room. Often I have felt that press conferences the world over have progressively become ceremonial events. The public, it would seem, can only be kept happy by quotations from the participants. Editors know this and, as a result, newspapers are filled with fatuous comments. Rarely, in my view, does a quotation enhance the value of a story. Journalists conceal their own shortcomings behind the gormless comments of someone obliged to say something on the spur of the moment. The pity is that there are so few journalists left who are able to write their own pieces and make it interesting enough without having to resort to using a participant to do it for them. Press conferences come and go and rarely do any good for anyone. It is their routine nature that is so irksome.

By the time Mike and I reached the clubhouse, David Lloyd was already sitting in front of the gathering journalists with an agitated look in his eyes. It was hot in that dining room and the atmosphere menacing. The situation called for a sensitive touch; a delicate late cut might have done the trick rather than a booming drive. The press conference began easily enough, and Atherton parried some obvious questions which were mainly concerned with his own form before Lloyd was brought into play and began by knocking the balls serenely back over the net.

Then, out of the blue and without warning, he, in response to an unassuming question, replied with some urgency in his voice: "We flippin' murdered them."

This was an unexpected answer and not much of a joke either. By now I had learnt that journalists when on duty are devoid of humour and very keen not to miss out on a news story for fear of incurring the wrath of their editors. For them, despite the absurdity of the comment, this was the moment for which they had waited patiently beneath the hot African sun. The pity was that it had been an exceptionally thrilling final day and the cricket, whilst not of the highest Test match standard, was compelling enough for all that. But now, with a few ill-considered words, it seemed that any chance of strengthening our friendship with our Zimbabwean hosts had been lost. It was a further setback to a tour that had never been blessed with much goodwill or joy.

In all this, poor David Lloyd had simply been let down by his own passion and commitment to the game and his team. His style and humour were completely misunderstood by Zimbabweans who had never come across someone so steeped in Accrington tradition, with an accent they could not decipher and ideas that were incomprehensible to them. There was undoubtedly a touch of genius in Lloyd's coaching style, but it was sad to see him go astray in Zimbabwe and lose so much support throughout the world of cricket.

This series of Test matches and one-day internationals should have served as a diversion from the persecution which had for so long dominated the country, a flash of joy amidst the current of fear. But politics were never far from the surface and took on a far more sinister nature than David Lloyd's outbursts.

Robert Mugabe visited the Harare Sports Club during the second Test match and spent several hours at the ground, during which he was presented to the teams amidst some ceremony. It was a symbolic gesture and one which left its mark upon players and administrators. Handshakes all round from Mugabe hardly put us in good spirits for the New Year, and – with the second Test also drawn – we managed to lose all three matches in the one-day series.

To perform so badly and lose with such ignominy in Zimbabwe left us without a lifeline. For all that, we should have oiled the wheels better off the field, and I can't help but think that I could have given a stronger lead to the rest of the squad.

It had been an ill-conceived and ill-judged tour with casualties on all sides. I wrote in my diary on New Year's Eve that I had never encountered a more impossible and unpleasant place to play cricket than Zimbabwe. Sadly a proud nation was disintegrating before our eyes and, without doubt, the cricket had become entangled in the mess.

27

NEW ZEALAND

From the hot and unhappy cauldron of Zimbabwe we flew to Auckland in New Zealand where the more gentle climate and lazy atmosphere offered us the chance to make a fresh start.

Not that it was easy to shake off the stigma of failure. Although we did receive a very friendly welcome in Auckland, despite touching down at 3.00 a.m. after our long flight around the world, I was determined to play a stronger hand on this leg of the tour, meet as many people as possible, make a few more speeches and generally fly the flag.

Despite the early hour the players, affected as they would be by the time change, set off into the darker parts of Auckland to celebrate their arrival in New Zealand with a drink. They were all wide awake and full of energy.

"Don't forget the press conference at ten o'clock," I shouted to Atherton as he set off. He gave me a wistful look and shuffled off with the other players.

Atherton, somewhat miraculously in the circumstances, did make it to the press conference, albeit with reddened eyes and an unshaven look. All went well for a bit. I said a few words at the start about how good it was to be in New Zealand and that we were determined to improve upon our recent performances in Zimbabwe. All pretty obvious stuff. But at this point, Michael Nicholson from ITN stood up and, clearly trying to match John Humphrys for hostility, vigorously attacked Atherton who was only just sober enough to understand what was happening. As so often it was the weak and cowardly nature of the press having a go at the strong, gifted but vulnerable.

To give him his due, Atherton gave as good as he got despite having so little ammunition up his sleeve. Blinking through bleary eyes, he saw off the onslaught as he might a particularly fiery burst from Ambrose or Walsh. It was an unsettling ten minutes and put paid to a sensible press conference which indeed folded up quickly after the Nicholson intervention.

We never saw Nicholson again. Presumably he went off elsewhere in the world to bully another unsuspecting victim. Meanwhile we set about our preparation for the first Test match by playing games in New Plymouth, Palmerston North and Hamilton. These were peaceful places to be staying and just right for a period of convalescence and recovery. Our two weeks up country appeared to be putting us in better shape to tackle the pressures of Test cricket again.

Back in Auckland, in overcast conditions and on a damp and well grassed pitch resembling Headingley on a grey day, Atherton bravely put New Zealand in to bat. At the end of the first day, on which our opponents had prospered against some wild and wayward English bowling, Atherton was asked at the press conference whether the pitch had provided the assistance he expected.

"We shall never know," he replied dryly and left it at that.

But things did pick up and, in reply to New Zealand's 390, England made 521 and so clearly had the upper hand.

During the evening of the fourth day and then before lunch on the fifth, England reduced New Zealand's second innings to 105 for eight and appeared to have clinched the match. At 142 for nine, with a lead of only 11 runs, it was surely all over for our opponents. Walking to the wicket was Danny Morrison. He had the dubious reputation of being the world's worst batsman with a record number of Test match ducks – 24. Surely just one straight ball would serve the purpose.

But a rapid end to the match was not forthcoming. Morrison, with his established partner Nathan Astle, kept the bowlers at bay. I shuffled about the ground uncomfortably, as well I might. I was conscious that, shortly before lunch, I had removed a case of Veuve Cliquot champagne from the boot of my car and put it in the fridge outside the dressing room. I was keen to be prepared for the great event.

For some of the afternoon I sat with Clive Radley, the MCC Head Coach, and his wife Linda as this ghastly saga unfolded. That was soothing because Clive, so used to encountering and staving off setbacks, mixed his words of hope with realism.

"You're stuffed," he said.

What I was most worried about was the champagne and how to remove it. Shortly before the end, with New Zealand's lead advancing out of control, I sneaked down to the fridge and, wrapping the drink up hurriedly in a team towel, carried it back to my car where it began to heat up again.

Once again a day of triumph had quickly become one of disaster. Was this a repeat of Zimbabwe all over again? Banana skins seemed to be lying about in wait for us.

The match ended with New Zealand well over 100 runs in the lead. We had run out of time. Astle had hit a century and, though we had bowled 133 balls at him, we never did get Morrison out. It was without doubt his finest hour with the bat and a very low moment for an England bowling attack that had begun to promise so much. More regrouping was needed.

Perhaps it is a good thing that in cricket there is never much time given to lick the wounds of failure. After a day's travel from Auckland we found ourselves in the peaceful outpost of Wanganui which, with its hilltop ground, should have provided England with perfect respite.

Unfortunately our response to the setback in Auckland was a feeble one against a very capable New Zealand 'A' team. Defeat by lunchtime on the fourth day once again proved that the ghosts of Zimbabwe were still haunting us. To get used to disaster is a dangerous habit but I was, if nothing else, beginning to become immune to batting collapses and bowling misfortunes and their unpleasant repercussions.

Dignity and self-belief were in short supply as we travelled by coach to Wellington for the second Test match. But here we encountered success at last. In damp and windy conditions England for once completely outplayed our opposition, winning by an innings. We had twice stumbled in sight of victory, first at Bulawayo and then at Auckland – Devon Loch in that famous Grand National comes to mind – and now we surprised New Zealand by simply using classic bowling skills on a green pitch with moisture always in the air. All of a sudden we had rediscovered the knack of winning. And so, triumphant and for once fulfilled, we flew to Christchurch where the players were rewarded for their success with a day off.

"Any plans for Christchurch?" Nasser Hussain enquired as we travelled in high spirits, morale lifting all the time.

"Yes," I said. "I've arranged a fishing trip. Why don't you come?"

To my surprise Nasser replied that he would. He thought it might be different and that he might even persuade some of the others to come too.

So the next day a party of ten set off in the mizzly rain for a day's fishing. I think it was mainly out of curiosity that Hussain, Irani, Silverwood, Knight and Emburey joined in while the rest of us – Atherton, Lloyd, Croft, Botham and Barclay – intended to fish the river. And these, we were assured, were not just any old fish. The majestic, fit and large salmon were now making their way up the rivers of the South Island in search of their spawning grounds in the upper reaches. The fishermen hoped rather unkindly to interrupt that journey.

We travelled in two land-rovers. It was not very comfortable. The wipers hissed as they swept the heavy rain from the windscreen and, by the time we reached the river some two hours later, enthusiasm for the trip was beginning to wane. One look at the surging torrent of water confirmed our worst fears. Dirty-brown, the river swirled menacingly downstream, carrying with it all manner of debris. Hopeless. Fishing was out of the question, so what next?

A crisis was averted when our generous guide for the day suggested that we made for the mountains where he thought the climate might be less turbulent and where at least we could find somewhere to enjoy the ample contents of the picnic hampers we had brought with us. The journey continued.

We drove high up into the hills until eventually we pulled off the main road and onto a rough farm track down which we bumped and disappeared into the mist. The views would have been spectacular but, with visibility down to fifty yards, this was not going to be a day for sightseeing. At last, after much discomfort, we found our destination for lunch, an isolated log-cabin set amongst pine trees in the middle of nowhere and in front of which was a small lake. It was believed to be full of fish. This was a remote spot, and the rain continued to pour down relentlessly. Without doubt we had distanced ourselves from the civilised world.

Despite the weather, fishing rods were assembled and it wasn't long before Emburey, Croft, Irani, Silverwood and Knight were taking it in turns to cast flies into the water. There were no fish to be seen. The fishermen returned to the hut and complained, as they would, that it was like bowling on a very good pitch with no sign of life or encouragement. Fishermen and bowlers have temperaments that are not altogether dissimilar.

Fishing was quickly given up as a bad job, and our intrepid hunters then turned their attention to shooting instead. A small group led by Irani and Silverwood set off into the mist with guns which had been borrowed.

Meanwhile, back in the log cabin, the more seasoned warriors, men of wisdom and experience, relaxed and put their feet up – not for them this cavorting about the sodden mountainside in the cold and wet. No, they preferred to tuck themselves inside where Nasser had successfully built up a blazing fire in front of which he, Atherton, Lloyd and Botham sizzled happily. All manner of food and drink emerged from the hampers. It was a massive feast which was eagerly devoured by the hungry and thirsty explorers. How we did enjoy that afternoon in the wild.

By the time the rest of the party had returned empty-handed from their hunting adventures (they had little experience of shooting wild boar), it was quite clear to them that those left behind had enjoyed a splendid lunch. The evidence surrounding us did little to conceal our happiness, while the jokes being told and games being played in front of the fire suggested that little, if any, of the excellent local wine had been wasted.

We travelled back to Christchurch, where the grey and dark conditions persisted, and looked forward to the final Test match. The weather, particularly English, reminded us of home while our recent victory in Wellington had put a smile on our faces and imbued us with a more confident sparkle for the deciding match.

Set to score 305 in the final innings to win, England's run chase and transformation in attitude was in sharp contrast to what we had become accustomed. At one stage we had lost six wickets for 231 and were taken to victory by a partnership of 76 between Crawley and Cork. But it was Atherton's courage and grit that was the main difference between the teams; he scored 212 runs in the match for once out, leading the team to a decisive victory in the series.

After all the troubles which Atherton had endured both in Zimbabwe and New Zealand, this result was a rich reward for his relentless determination and stubborn single-mindedness. He was dismissive of the press, excepting one or two of them, and tended to save up his charm and humour for a few selected friends. He treated the many fools on tour with disdain. These were not always ideal leadership attributes, but few would deny that Atherton was a tough customer, one whom you would be happy to have on your side.

The final three hours or so of that match in Christchurch were agony for me. As manager I was powerless to help.

I spent much of my time downstairs in the dressing room, removed from the live action but kept in touch by way of a small television with snowy reception. Players trooped in and out from time to time, and the atmosphere became increasingly unsettled when a wicket fell. Would a bat be hurled about the room in anger and frustration?

As Crawley and Cork settled into what turned out to be the conclusive partnership, nobody moved or changed places. Cricketers are instinctively a superstitious bunch. I passed some of the time, as the score slowly advanced, arranging a day's fishing for Atherton and Croft on the Hope River about three hours away, convinced that this would be good for them and their tormented minds as well as for me. Both players had had an outstanding match and earned this special treat. It also kept me occupied during the final overs.

Both Atherton and Croft are probably even more enthusiastic about their fishing than their cricket. Croft fishes the great Welsh rivers, his special favourite the Teifi, for sea trout for which rivers in Wales are famous. For Atherton it was early days still although he had successfully caught his first salmon in Scotland. Also one or two trips to the Tweed had been rumoured to be successful.

Now here we were on New Zealand's South Island and fishing a great river, creeping up and down its banks in pursuit of trout. We peered into the water hopefully but for quite a while saw no fish.

"There's one just out from the bank," I said pointing self-consciously so as not to disturb the water.

"No, it's only weed," came the gloomy reply.

I was not so sure and suggested gently that it might be worth someone having a cast if only to prove me wrong. It was not long before Atherton had his fly, a hairy green thing, swishing about on the end of his line and landing on the water. It floated down not far from the patch of weed and quite impressively too. The fly at least sat up and looked life-like.

It was at this point that I had a Jeremy Fisher moment. From the depths of the river appeared a large shadow, slightly green and well-spotted. It hung as if suspended in the water just beneath the fly with its tail waving, well-balanced and sorely tempted. Then it lifted its head and sipped the fly off the surface of the water.

Atherton, with a shout, lifted his rod with some vigour and drove the hook into the poor fish's mouth. The fight was on. And it went on seemingly for ages. The fish was large, fit, strong and wild. A fine specimen. Oh for more cricketers with similar attributes. Line screamed off the reel and it took off downstream into the rough water. Atherton, from the bank, pursued his quarry and athletically vaulted rocks that stood in his way. The rest of us followed at a discreet distance, not wishing to disturb the concentration of our captain turned fisherman.

As the fish began to tire, I crept in closer to the edge of the stream and, with landing net in my hand, tried to find a suitable backwater into which Atherton could steer the fish to the bank. It was a tense business, just like the recent Test series. The fish, beginning to circle as exhaustion set in, took off again into the middle of the stream at the sight of me and my net. This tends to happen, but it was still a ghastly moment. There is nothing worse than holding the net with the responsibility for the safe landing of a great prize. The fear of failure is intense and the consequences awful.

Eventually the big fish was drawn in close enough for me to fulfil my duties successfully. Atherton had landed a magnificent brown trout which, accompanied by a ripple of applause from our small party, made our trip to New Zealand even more worthwhile. We weighed the fish then and there. Seven and a half pounds.

That same evening Atherton's trout was brought to my room in the hotel, accompanied by vegetables and salad, and it fed most of the players whose scepticism towards fishing was diminished somewhat by the excellence of the feast.

With the Test matches now finished and the excitement wearing thin, we had to brace ourselves for five one-day internationals. We won the first of them in Christchurch, largely due to an inspired piece of bowling on a worn pitch by Phil Tufnell. Tufnell was not a man entirely at home with the rigours of touring; he would suffer the jitters, especially when confronted by an aeroplane. But he had stuck to his guns during this long tour and bowled with increasing confidence throughout many extended days in the field. A funny man too, on his day, and often able to see the lighter side of a disaster.

The second match too was won, rather fortuitously, after a rain interruption revised the overs very much in our favour. The game does have a fickle way of rewarding you unexpectedly. So we flew off to Napier in the dangerous and improbable position of leading the one-day series by two wins to nil and so seemingly on the front foot.

Complacency can set in. In Napier we came within a cat's whisker of clinching the series when eight runs were needed from the final over and just two from the last two balls. England made only one and the match was tied. Dormy two.

The fourth match, rain affected and consequently unbalanced, should have been won by England too but, following the uncanny pattern of the last three months, was squandered at the last gasp and lost by nine runs in a low scoring game in the course of which Nick Knight's finger was badly broken.

In the end the series petered out rather tepidly in Wellington by which time England had run out of strength and stamina and slid to a 28-run defeat. The trophy was shared with honours even.

The highlight of the final day came during the interval when Ian Botham joined more than thirty New Zealand police officers and had his hair shaved from his head to raise £50,000 for the Child Cancer Foundation. One-day cricket has progressively become filled with such exploits and stunts, but at least this one was in a good cause.

So it was that the tour reached its rather tame conclusion. The players were tired and had, to some extent, been put through the mill – mostly self-inflicted. The squad had not been chosen with compatibility in mind; not enough of them appreciated the challenges and responsibilities of travelling on an overseas tour. They were not without ability, but since 1997 I sense that selectors and coaches have been more discerning not only about the skill of the players but also the type of people involved. This can make a huge difference.

As it was, I as tour manager had no influence upon the selection of personnel. "Just give me the raw material, and I'll try to make things tick." But I often wonder whether I could have done more to give the players a lead and guide them on their way. To chastise or cajole, it is always a tricky balance.

With the smallest amount of luck and extra skill, four out of the five Test matches that winter would have been won as well as the one-day series in New Zealand. But our performances in the one-day matches in Zimbabwe will forever remain a scar on English cricket and its values.

It was the last winter I toured with an England team.

28

MARY-LOU

I know of no sport that punishes failure as ruthlessly and unforgivingly as cricket does, and particularly for the poor batsman whose entry and exit is so embarrassingly public and dramatic at whatever level the game is played. Dismissal is a shock, a humiliation, like getting the sack. Irreversible. One moment you're batting, full of hope, but then in an instant those hopes are dashed. A small error is punished with unjustified harshness. Sometimes execution is accompanied by the fielding team shouting at you with their appeal. The umpire's cold stare and uncompromisingly raised finger signifies death, the end of another innings. It's all over. Back to the pavilion, head bowed, a whispered good luck to the incoming batsman, respectful silence from team mates or small crowd and then departure to the dressing-room for a period of mourning. Head in hands, the fatal ball is replayed mentally in slow motion while future batsmen strap on their equipment. These days misery is accompanied by the sound of ripping velcro.

Recovery can be quick; a cup of tea helps. I'm not actually dead, wounded maybe, pride hurt but not a mortal blow. There's always tomorrow, a second innings perhaps. One fact is inescapable, though, for the ordinary, gritty and determined cricketer; failures vastly outnumber successes so it is as well to be prepared.

That is where, all those years ago, the airing cupboard came in. Although I was too young to realise it, I was in a way preparing myself for setbacks, the shock and humiliation of failure. That was then, over forty years ago.

"When I was a child, I spoke as a child, I understood as a child, I thought as a child: but when I became a man, I put away childish things."

I began to move on after being stumped by a girl off a wide ball on the banks of the River Cherwell in Oxford. It dawned on me that I needed God's help, a close ally, if I was to cope with life and with the agony of cricket in particular. So prayer replaced ritual and became for me far more important to my preparation than the manic turbulence of frantic training regimes. A cup of tea and a quiet moment did more for my batting than anything else. The strength of my faith eased me through the periods of woe and put the brakes on during those rare moments of elation.

That we are all going to die is the one great certainty about our life on earth. To some extent the way we behave is dominated by our ultimate demise. Life for many is a struggle against adversity, sometimes with the unwelcome interference of power and greed. But ultimately we are controlled by our weakness, mortality and death – the final and most glorious failure of all.

When Mary-Lou, my wife, died late on in 2000 I was sort of ready for it. But only sort of. The prospects hadn't been good, but she was getting better and due to come out of hospital on the day she died. Despite her frailty she was strong in spirit, so much so that the previous evening I went off with her blessing and with Theo, aged 11, to speak to a church dinner in Cirencester. Mary-Lou died soon after I finished my speech. I wasn't even there.

You'll find that cricketers aren't often there when their wives need them. The lot of the wives and girlfriends is not a very happy one. Abandoned for weeks on end during the summer and frequently for long periods of the winter, mentally out of touch for much of the time too, the wives have a wretched time. They are left to pick up the shattered pieces, bringing up the children as single parents for parts of every year.

For me days of failure far outnumbered those of success. There were no mobile telephones back in the '70s and '80s. I would simply push the door open when I got home and deliver the grim news. Little wonder that rain was such a precious commodity and so much sought after. It eased the pressure.

Mary-Lou was always there, in the earlier days with Georgie and much later Theo too. It was helpful that her level of expectation diminished as she came to understand cricket. She coped with a strange cricketer, too, whose bouts of depression muddled up with occasional manic interludes would have tested a saint. She never seemed surprised by all of this, almost proud in a funny sort of way.

If cricket does nothing more for us in life, it does at least prepare us a little for the worst, for death. The countless days of failure are responsible for that. Prayers provided comfort as indeed they did when Mary-Lou died. Lest we ever forget: death comes as a very fast ball and is decisive.

29

THE NEXT CHAPTER

Whatever way you look at it and however brave you might be (and many are very), the aftershock of death strikes right at the heart of our existence and is hard to bear. Initially there is too much going on, little time for self-pity and gloom. No, that comes later when all goes quiet. I think it's the loneliness that grips the soul most severely, collecting Theo from school and returning together to a silent house, dark and rather cold in January.

"Turn all the lights on," Mary-Lou's mother advised. "It helps." And it did, but it didn't improve the taste of jam sandwiches, baked beans and pasta. My cooking was limited, but Theo was hungry.

These were dark days. I kept taking the pills, of course, and the doctor prescribed a few more for good measure. "No medals for being a hero," he said, "and resisting the product of medical research." I hated taking pills and from time to time threw them away in disgust. Total despair took its course, and I was quickly reunited with my medication. I wasn't so much down in the dumps as bewildered. I needed to get back on course.

Two things came to my rescue. Paul Parker rang me up. After his distinguished cricket career with Sussex and later Durham, he had for some while been teaching at Tonbridge School in Kent where he was a housemaster. "Why don't you do some writing?" he said over the telephone. "And, to give you an incentive, I'll arrange dinner with Keith Blackmore, the *Times* sports editor. He lives in Brighton and loves cricket."

So, about two weeks later, in a little Spanish restaurant in the Lanes in Brighton, we had dinner together and a real laugh too. It was probably mid-February by now but, apart from a few early daffodils, not much sign of spring in the air. All the same Keith gave me a small project to think about. Coinciding with the Australian tour of England, with the Ashes at stake, he asked me to submit a few articles to *The Times* based around Sussex's quest for the championship twenty years earlier in

1981 and also to remind the readers (hopefully there would be some) of England's remarkable comeback and victory in that great Ashes series. Botham's year.

I was thrilled to have a go at this and even more so when I discovered that Keith and the *Times* sports staff liked my stuff. They decided to print a weekly column on Saturdays throughout the season under the heading 'That Summer'. It gave me something to get my teeth into. I wrote the pieces early in the morning in long-hand (typing has never been a talent), had the product put on disc by a friendly neighbour whereupon Theo and I corrected and rewrote bits before he sent them off to *The Times* via our computer, which I couldn't work but fortunately he could. Teamwork is always essential even when writing.

In all, we did about twenty pieces together and it kept me going all summer at the end of which, with the help of Stephen Chalke, they were turned into a book, *The Appeal of the Championship*. That was fun to do as well and was published in June 2002. As a result of Paul's intervention, I had discovered I liked writing. I now just wished I had read more books when I was younger. Relentless hours in the nets and on the cricket field had put paid to that.

There was a second event that helped to get me back on the tracks early in 2001. About ten days after Mary-Lou's death, Colin Cowdrey, who had become one of my closest friends through the Arundel project, also died. He had had a stroke back in July and was gradually recovering when suddenly his heart gave out. Much has already been written about Colin both as a cricketer and administrator, but I prefer to think of him in his slippers and scruffy clothes at home with dogs clambering all over him. He was a great friend, and I missed his frequent telephone calls (voice always fading away at the end) and many notes, usually scribbled on postcards.

One evening in February there was a knock on the stable door of our cottage in Amberley. It was Graham Cowdrey. He asked me if I would like to read a poem at his father's memorial service in Westminster Abbey at the end of March, a poem written some years earlier by William Douglas-Home, "A glorious game say we…" This was a great honour and a pleasure, even if somewhat terrifying. But it gave me something to think about, and I rehearsed it diligently with Theo as my tutor and critic. He can still recite the poem off by heart today.

The great day arrived. I don't think there was a spare place anywhere to be found in the Abbey – side aisles, nave and choir stalls all choc-a-bloc. I was seated in the choir where, although I hadn't got a clear view of the Abbey's awesome majesty, I was close to the great organ from which Elgar's *Nimrod* could be heard as the congregation filed in and said their prayers.

Sitting next to me as I nervously fingered my order of service, which included a witty musical interlude written by Tim Rice and based on Gilbert and Sullivan's *Mikado*, was the former Prime Minister Edward Heath. He looked old and tired which indeed he was. With a sad and slightly disappointed, resigned look in his eyes, it struck me how lonely it must have been to handle affairs of state without the comfort and succour of close companionship. Amidst his many talents, music and sailing being the most prominent, the empty void must have been stark when the miners were at their most belligerent in the early seventies. Later, I presume, there was no one to help him overcome his bitterness and irritation towards Margaret Thatcher's vastly different style of leadership. His had been a brilliant career but both unfulfilled and almost certainly consumed by loneliness. We made quite a pair sitting in the choir stalls that morning and never spoke to each other, either. That might have spoilt things.

Colin's service was a small turning point. I derived much comfort from it. Christopher Cowdrey and John Major in their addresses both spoke with wit and charm which captured the essence of Colin and enchanted the congregation. David Sheppard, Bishop of Liverpool, led the prayers. Strangely, you might think, I have always rather enjoyed funerals and memorial services, now more commonly known as services of celebration or thanksgiving. Admittedly, funerals recently have become somewhat 'dumbed down' in an attempt, I imagine, to ease the burden of death. This I don't particularly object to except when an address becomes something more akin to an after-dinner speech, without the drink of course.

I think on balance I prefer funerals – not all of them – to weddings. They are generally more satisfactory and conclusive, and the party afterwards is often every bit as good as at a wedding, not so long and without the disco and dancing. Give me a good funeral any day.

Be that as it may, there was still much sadness and melancholy to be overcome, and travelling home on the bus with Theo from Colin's service there was a good deal of emptiness in our hearts and a lot of convalescence still to be completed. But we had at least made a start.

By 2003 things were looking up. The Arundel project was moving strongly in the right direction. Sussex had just signed Mushtaq Ahmed, and I had met someone called Renira. In fact, I had met her long before, in 1975, but, let's face it, quite a lot of water flows under the bridge in twenty-seven years.

And so towards the end of the year it all began to come together. Quite remarkably, after more than a hundred years of trying, Sussex won the cherished county championship for the first time in its distinguished history, and soon afterwards I married Renira in a ceremony in Chichester that was not quite so long and drawn out. Then lunch at Bailiff's Court Hotel in Climping was followed by a five-day honeymoon in Venice. One way and another, September 2003 was a good month and certainly came a long way towards compensating for the darker times.

Rarely am I rash enough to make a prophecy, but at the end of *The Appeal of the Championship* I wrote, 'Sussex will win the championship some day and the joy will be great when the time comes.' Little did I know when I wrote those words that I only had two years to wait.

Often in life I find it is the waiting that makes for the most treasured moments. Each year at Hove successive chairmen would wish us luck before the start of a new season, and they really meant it. "This is our year," they would say with the cheerful optimism reserved for pre-season. It never was. All they really wanted in life was to win the county championship – then they would die happy. Now they are all dead, of course, and so we can only speculate upon how they would have felt.

And wasn't it odd, and in some way ironic, that after all those years it should be a slow bowler who in 2003 finally did the trick? Ironic, because Sussex in its history has never fully understood the nature of spin bowling, using such tactics more often as an afterthought than part of the plan. Of course, there was much more to the team than just Mushtaq Ahmed; more or less the same group of players pulled it off again in 2006 and 2007 to form the most successful short era in the club's history. It somehow came rather out of the blue and was all the more thrilling for it.

30

A DAY IN THE GARDEN

Looking out from the kitchen door and if I crane my neck quite far to the left, I can see most of our land, such as it is. But what I don't see are very many flower beds and certainly no vegetables. Set amidst the stern landscape of solid clay, rock-hard in summer, we can't be doing with pretty borders and showy shrubs. Ours is a low-maintenance garden; we have plenty of lawn for football and cricket and generally ragging about on.

This does not mean that our life is totally devoid of flowers; that would be far from the truth. We are particularly strong when it comes to spring flowers, which with global warming are now with us around Christmas time or soon afterwards. Snowdrops are first to arrive although nowadays they have become increasingly muddled up with the daffodils while primroses and their leaves are pushing through in early January too. It's something of a waste really because so much of the spring is now finished before we have woken up to it.

The bluebells are spectacular and each year produce a hazy carpet in the wooded end of the garden, where there are violets too. The wonderful thing about all this is that we have to do so little about it other than to thank God and admire His creation, taking time to appreciate what we've got. All too often, I find, too much activity is a substitute for achievement.

What with the planes and the trains, it could be argued that to sit with a drink in the garden is not entirely restful. The sounds of nature are constantly interrupted. Aeroplanes fly overhead every three or four minutes when the wind is in the east, but they keep me in touch with travel and travellers. I feel a warmth inside me, knowing that other people are fastening their seat belts, will have luggage and customs to deal with, and airports to face. By comparison, it is very good to watch them flying over.

Trains are not the same at all. I love them, even the modern ones which contentedly rattle along the Arun Valley. The train is a pleasing method of travelling – occasionally clean, usually quick and remarkably punctual. I watch them from the garden and very rarely does one disappoint me and keep me waiting, often heralding its presence with a tuneless toot from the horn. The sound of the train in the distance is for me every bit as important as the sound of the cuckoo; it is constant throughout the year.

Five years ago, when we bought our house, there was a pond in the middle of a wooded area towards the bottom of the garden, which is overlooked by the South Downs directly north of Chanctonbury Ring. The pond is still there but sometimes only just, the source of both pain and joy in about equal measure. It has no stream, not even a trickle, running through it and so it relies on rain to supplement the meagre amount of spring water that bubbles out of the ground. Foolishly I have stocked this small pond with goldfish and, as I write, there is a drought, and I fear my fish have only limited life expectancy. They live, let's be honest, in a puddle.

Despite this, the pond is a haven for water plants and wild life. Surrounded by reeds, there is enough cover to conceal rabbits which, from time to time, Comet, our eleven-year-old Jack Russell terrier, flushes out amidst much commotion. In his hey-day he may have caught the odd one but now the rabbits are quite safe, even if irritated to be disturbed. For Comet, though, it is still a very good game.

I have once seen a stoat concealed in a drain pipe at one end of the pond, doubtless with an eye for the rabbits too – though far more deadly, of course, than Comet.

The pond is full of newts which rise to the surface like submarines and then return to the mud at the bottom. They are prolific unlike snakes which I only rarely see. That is not to say that they too are not plentiful, but they are shy and hold their counsel. Grass snakes love the water and enjoy a swim, their tiny heads leading the way, their thin bodies following with a wavy stroke. Their colouring is beautiful, a rich combination of yellows and greens, their appearance most welcome but all too rare.

Not so far away as the pond is the chicken run. This we built four years ago with an electric wire encircling the plot for fear of the many foxes in the area. We love our chickens, all bantams, and currently look after 12 of them. They lead a life of luxury and uninterrupted happiness exemplified by the very high standard of accommodation to which they have become accustomed.

Mr Knightley is our only cockerel and most senior bird; the hens follow his lead out of respect and duty. A year or two ago Mr Knightley's inclination to perform in a frisky and suggestive way towards his girls was not inconsiderable. He would come at them quite suddenly from sideways and, when they were least expecting action, would pounce on them for what I suppose was a moment of passion. But now in his old age all this tomfoolery has gone and the hens can peck away at the grass without fear of disturbance. They certainly don't appear to be much bothered.

The chickens seem to eat more or less anything and, having the run of the garden, frequently invade the kitchen when the door is open; they particularly like Comet's food. They have been known to explore further; Popeye was once found prancing up and down the piano keys, composing some modern music, while Tuffy sat sedately on the sofa.

The magical thing about hens is that they lay eggs – sometimes. Despite a long barren period in the winter for which we forgive them, come spring and it's a different story. Eggs are littered about the garden in unexpected places. The dog basket in the garage was a favourite spot for a bit; the log shed, under bushes and trees, and even occasionally in the henhouse.

Every now and then we have a drama. A brown dog got into the garden once; it ate one chicken and frightened two others to death. Amidst all the feathers and hullabaloo there wasn't much to be done. It was a sad day, but a week or so later we visited Molly who rears chickens nearby and brought the numbers up again.

On another occasion Renira, whose passion for chickens is even greater than mine was having tea with her friend Lucy when, all of a sudden, Lucy's puppy, Trumpet, forgot himself and went on the rampage in the garden. The hens scattered to all corners. Trumpet trotted back into the kitchen as if nothing had happened but, dangling suggestively from the corner of his mouth, there was a feather.

Long into the evening, Renira and I searched for the missing hens, aided by the feeble light of a torch and by Comet whose ability to sniff out a chicken exceeded that of us humans. One by one the hens were found, one on top of the car and several others out of bounds on the other side of the fence. Remarkably, no damage had been done and Trumpet was forgiven. It had been a narrow squeak.

Our house is surrounded by tall trees, mostly oaks, which provide the wild birds with sanctuary and a vantage point from which to sing and take stock of their surroundings. They compose a lot of music, with the volume turned up particularly high at around 5.30 am. I lie in bed and listen to the bird song without being able to make up my mind whether to get up for an early cup of tea or slide back into an unconscious state. Birds give us endless pleasure. We hardly ever see anything rare, but the common garden birds descend upon our nut supply with relish. They have become our friends.

Three years ago we got a surprise when a pair of flycatchers arrived from Africa to nest in a box we had nailed to an oak tree by the garden fence. They sang their little tune incessantly and before long produced a family of four with hungry mouths to feed. They took it in turns to search for food – flies presumably – and for a while this happy unit went from strength to strength, until one day the cat, Myrtle, got one of the parents and left it half-eaten on the kitchen floor.

It was a very bad moment. Renira was inconsolable. Of course I realise that cats can't help themselves when it comes to birds, but we were now left with the responsibility of coping with a single parent family and all that that entails. The remaining adult bird was rushed off its feet – whether it was Mr or Mrs Flycatcher, I know not – bringing up the family alone. As with humans, feeding and education were the main challenges. Both were successfully accomplished, and by

July the nest was abandoned and we assumed that the long journey back to Africa was under way.

My day in the garden would not be complete without further mention of the rabbits. We are surrounded by these common little furry mammals, and mostly they are brown in colour and uninteresting. But every now and then, down by the old air-raid shelter in the bluebell wood by the pond, a black rabbit appears. He's a brave little chap and generally unflustered by mankind. Even Comet treats him with a little extra respect.

Instinct tells me that this chapter and indeed this book should now come to an end. From time to time we all need to spend a day in the garden, in powerful contrast to the confinement of the airing cupboard.

INDEX

Not including John Barclay and his close family

Fairfield Books

Fairfield Books is a specialist publisher of cricket books.

The following of its titles are still in print:

John Barclay, *Life Beyond The Airing Cupboard*
Stephen Chalke, *The Way It Was – Glimpses of English Cricket's Past*
Simon Lister, *Supercat – The Authorised Biography of Clive Lloyd*
Stephen Chalke & Derek Hodgson,
 No Coward Soul – The Remarkable Story of Bob Appleyard (paperback)
Peter Walker, *It's Not Just Cricket*
Stephen Chalke, *Tom Cartwright – The Flame Still Burns*
Stephen Chalke,
 Runs in the Memory – County Cricket in the 1950s (paperback)
Douglas Miller, *Charles Palmer – More than just a Gentleman*
Stephen Chalke, *Ken Taylor – Drawn to Sport*
David Foot, *Fragments of Idolatry – From 'Crusoe' to Kid Berg*
Stephen Chalke, *Guess My Story – The Life and Opinions of Keith Andrew*
Stephen Chalke, *Five Five Five – Holmes and Sutcliffe in 1932* (paperback)

The following are now out of print:

John Barclay, *The Appeal of the Championship – Sussex in the Summer of 1981*
Stephen Chalke, *Caught in the Memory – County Cricket in the 1960s*
David Foot, *Harold Gimblett, Tormented Genius of Cricket*
Stephen Chalke, *One More Run – with Bryan 'Bomber' Wells*
Douglas Miller, *Born to Bowl – The Life and Times of Don Shepherd*
Stephen Chalke,
 At the Heart of English Cricket – The Life and Memories of Geoffrey Howard
David Foot & Ivan Ponting, *Sixty Summers – Somerset Cricket since the War*
Stephen Chalke, *A Summer of Plenty – George Herbert Hirst in 1906*

If you would like more details of any of these, or would like to be placed on the mailing list for future publications, please contact:
Fairfield Books, 17 George's Road, Bath BA1 6EY
telephone 01225-335813